What?
AND GIVE UP SHOW BUSINESS?

What?
AND GIVE UP SHOW BUSINESS?

JAMES HAMPTON

TCU
Press

FORT WORTH, TEXAS

Library of Congress Cataloging-in-Publication Data

Names: Hampton, Jim, author.
Title: What? and give up show business? / James Hampton.
Description: Fort Worth, Texas : TCU Press, [2020] | Summary: "What? And Give Up Show Business?
  is the hilarious autobiography of James Hampton, who for over fifty years has been one of the
  most familiar faces in television and film. A wonderful slice of life in Hollywood told through the
  personal stories of one of its most prolific actors, this book will appeal to nostalgia buffs, classic
  film and television aficionados, fans of celebrity autobiographies and biographies, and people who
  just enjoy a good laugh and great storytelling. This enchanting memoir also includes some of the
  author's favorite recipes, which are woven into stories about such show business icons as Doris
  Day, Clint Eastwood, and Michael J. Fox. Never-before-seen photographs of Hampton and his
  friends, who happen to be some of the world's favorite entertainers, pepper this jewel of a tale
  chronicling life in La-La Land. Everyone who loves classic television and films will enjoy What?
  And Give Up Show Business? -- JAMES HAMPTON has had a long career as an actor, writer, and
  director that has spanned more than fifty years. Notable roles in movies such as The Longest Yard
  and Sling Blade, as well as in popular television shows from F Troop to Murder, She Wrote, made
  James Hampton "That Guy" whose actual name is just on the tip of your tongue. A favorite guest
  of Johnny Carson, Hampton had over thirty appearances on The Tonight Show. He also worked
  behind the scenes as a writer, director, and producer on many successful sitcoms such as Evening
  Shade, Sister Sister, Smart Guy, Boston Common, and Grace Under Fire"-- Provided by publisher.
Identifiers: LCCN 2020026936 | ISBN 9780875657615 (cloth)
Subjects: LCSH: Hampton, Jim. | Actors--United States--Biography. | Television producers and direc-
  tors--United States--Biography. | Motion picture industry--California--Los Angeles--Anecdotes. |
  LCGFT: Autobiographies. | Anecdotes. | Cookbooks.
Classification: LCC PN2287.H1794 A3 2020 | DDC 791.4302/8092 [B]--dc23
LC record available at https://lccn.loc.gov/2020026936

TCU Box 298300
Fort Worth, Texas 76129
817.257.7822
www.prs.tcu.edu
To order books: 1.800.826.8911

Cover and Text Design by Preston Thomas

To my wife Mary, who makes life fun.
I'm glad you said "Yes."

CONTENTS

FOREWORD

James Hampton, award-winning actor/director/ writer/producer of stage, screen, and television, has penned a hilarious memoir about his life in the entertainment industry. *What? And Give Up Show Business?* gives us more than a glimpse into what happens backstage, in the makeup trailers and around the craft service tables of some of the greatest movies and television shows of our time.

An A-list character actor with more than thirty *Tonight Show* appearances, Jim has seen and heard it all in a nearly fifty-year love affair with show business and its denizens. Johnny Carson once made his audience pledge to "remember the name of James Hampton," a guy he called one of the most recognized faces in television and film, and it's true.

A master of the well-told story and memorable punch line, Jim's memoir is loaded with laughs and heart in a pitch-perfect rendering of Hollywood and the vibrant personalities that inhabit it.

Have you ever wondered what Johnny Carson and other talk show hosts were saying to their guests as they went to commercial break? How did Adrienne Barbeau save Jim's life? Would Lee J. Cobb wear a two-dollar hat? How long did it take Michael J. Fox in the make-up chair to become a *Teen Wolf*?

Jim's stories take you behind the scenes of your favorite films, sitcoms, and television shows with stars like Jimmy Stewart, Pat Boone, Doris Day, Rock Hudson, Roy Rogers, Jack Lemmon, Michael Douglas, Jane Fonda, James Garner, Burt Reynolds, George Hamilton, Billy Bob Thornton, and Clint Eastwood, just to name a few.

Nevertheless, even with the tremendous success he has achieved, Jim gleefully compares himself to the guy who sweeps up after the elephants in the circus parade. When asked why he didn't "quit and get a better job," his answer was always the same: "What? And give up show business?"

—ADRIANA TRIGIANI

ONE
CUTE KID

Little Jimmy Hampton at three-and-a-half years old. *Author Collection.*

I didn't start out as a cute kid. I was always attracting attention to myself for all the wrong reasons. For instance, people stared at my upper lip. It wasn't enough that I was small, sickly, and had no athletic ability. I also had warts on my upper lip. They just started appearing until there was a flock of them. The other kids would laugh and say I had kissed a frog. Very funny.

One day, my mother took me to the Freeman Clinic about another problem. It could have been earaches, rheumatic fever, leg cramps, or a few other things, but while we were there the doctor asked if I had anything else I needed seeing to. I pointed to my upper lip. He nodded gravely and began to rummage through his desk drawer.

"Now where did I put that magic cream? Ah, here it is."

He had my full attention. He produced a small jar of topical ointment. Then, he leaned over and very seriously told me how I must use this special medicine.

"Jimmy, I want you to put this cream on your upper lip every night for one whole month. Do you think you can do that?"

I nodded dumbly.

"Now, you may not see any improvement for the first couple of weeks. In fact, you may not see much improvement right up until the last night you apply this. But don't worry, that's just the way this stuff works. When you wake up the next morning, every last one of those warts will have disappeared."

And that's just what happened. I woke up one morning a month later and they were gone. Later, my mother told me she had asked the doctor what that miracle ointment was. He told her it was cold cream. It was the same stuff that women of that era put on their faces at bedtime. It worked because he convinced me it would.

It didn't matter. The day those warts disappeared was the day I started my career as a cute kid. I went from wishing I could be invisible one day to wanting to be noticed the next. Sometimes it got me into trouble, but I couldn't help it. With my newfound cuteness, I never failed to seize an opportunity to get a laugh. Many times it seemed inappropriate to others but not to me. Back then it was called "showing off." There was a fine line between showing off and being a "show-off." A show-off was smug and conceited. Conceited was just about the worst thing you could call another person when I was growing up.

The first speaking role I had was as George Washington in a May Day pageant at Reagan Elementary. My mother, who could create anything on her portable Singer sewing machine, made me a costume of black knee breeches and a swallowtail coat. She fashioned a knockout white wig out of cotton batting with a black bow in the back and sewed white lace on the front of my shirt and at the cuffs. Dad tied a pair of buckles on my shoes. When I saw myself in the mirror, I looked like a one-dollar bill. I couldn't believe how handsome and presidential I looked!

1

The show was going very well that night. Carol Lamb played Miss Liberty. When she turned on her flashlight torch, she received applause. Then Vernon Knight, the biggest boy in the class, stormed onstage carrying a small tree.

He was frowning when he uttered, "George Washington, come out here."

That was my cue. It was time for George's entrance. I strode regally (or, I guess, democratically) into the spotlight.

"Yes, Father?"

"Did you cut down my cherry tree?"

I showed him my hatchet and said, "I cannot tell a lie, Father. It was I."

I slumped in remorse. A little too much remorse, as it turned out. When I slumped, my wig fell off. The children were so delighted and excited they began to laugh. I was flustered and accidentally put the wig back on backwards. Now the adults were laughing. I turned away from the audience and took another bow to Miss Liberty, who almost dropped her torch. I threw up my coat in the back as I bent from the waist and walked around like Groucho Marx. I blew on the little ponytail with the black ribbon on it, then I lifted it up, peered out at the audience, and did a big Red Skelton take. There were screams of laughter. Carol Lamb began to tremble so intensely that her crown tilted and slipped over one eye, provoking even more hilarity. I turned back around and did my Groucho Marx walk. None of us could say our lines for all the laughing.

Finally, Miss Paar struck up "God Bless America" and the show was over. It was the most wonderful feeling I had ever experienced.

Here I was in the limelight with everyone looking at me and enjoying my antics.

No one was chanting, "You kissed a frog, you kissed a frog!"

I spotted my older brother, Blake, in the audience. He wasn't laughing. He wasn't even smiling.

Jealous, I thought.

In my Aunt Blanche's Plymouth on the way back to Southern Crest, things were pretty quiet. I didn't notice, though, as I was still flushed with success. I had made a fatal error for an actor. If your family and friends aren't raving about your performance, then under no circumstances do you ask them for a reaction. I didn't know that. I was in the second grade.

"Did you like the show?" I asked.

'43 SCHOOL DAYS '44
JOHN H. REAGAN

Bad hair day in elementary school. *Author Collection.*

Halloween in South Oak Cliff, 1940s. *Author Collection.*

Aunt Blanche did the talking for the family, "The show was fine. At least, part of it."

"What about me? Did you like my part?"

There was a pause. I assumed my Aunt Blanche (a lawyer, later a judge and Woman of the Year) was searching for the right adjective. Words like colossal, stupendous, and hilarious came to mind.

"Jimmy, I thought you were embarrassing. You certainly embarrassed our family."

There were grunts of approval from the other passengers, now my former family.

"I thought you were just being a big show-off. I don't think the father of our country would act like a conceited buffoon, prancing around like somebody from *Duck Soup.*"

At least she got my Groucho.

More nods and icy stares from the strangers I was riding with. My head began to reel. I was having trouble breathing. Aunt Blanche had murdered me with "show-off" and buried me with "conceited." It was a double-barreled blast of familial rock salt aimed at my seven-year-old actor's ego that was right on target and still stings my memory. If there was a lesson to be learned that warm spring night in the back of that Plymouth, it escaped me. I stayed mad at Aunt Blanche until I was well into the fifth grade.

(Left) Mom and Dad in the 1970s. (Bottom left) Our old house, 1950s. (Bottom right) Reading the funny papers with our dog Butch. *Author Collection.*

MAMA

I was doing my chores on a spring Saturday morning. Mama was sweeping. I was dusting the piano for the second time because, according to her, I hadn't done it right the first time. I was late for our softball game with the Methodists and my pal Lefty was pacing outside waiting for me to emerge. Mother began her litany as she swept. I was standing on the piano bench carefully wiping under crocheted doilies and around about sixty pictures of family, as well as a black, crouching, shiny, ceramic panther with evil green glass eyes that always seemed to be mocking me.

She was at the point where she said that she and Dad were unable to sleep for worrying about me. She wasn't sure if they were going to ship me off to military school or hand me over to the nuns. She had given birth to my little brother, Dan, at St. Joseph's Hospital, and she knew that the nuns there had creeped me out. Then the awful thing happened. Somehow, to my surprise, I heard the words "shut up" escape from my thirteen-year-old mouth.

There was a moment of suspended animation. I stopped breathing. Birds stopped chirping. I immediately thought, *Wait, maybe she didn't hear me.* Right then, her broom caught me with full force above my left ear. I did a half gainer off the piano bench and bounced into the wall. I was unhurt, but I thought maybe I could gain some ground with good old-fashioned guilt.

"Mama! You clubbed me with the broom! You could have killed me!"

She looked me square in the eyes and calmly and carefully said, "You'd better be glad I wasn't ironing."

My Mama's Porcupine Meatballs

INGREDIENTS FOR MEATBALLS

1¼ pounds ground beef
½ cup of raw long grain rice
¼ teaspoon black pepper
½ cup dry breadcrumbs
½ teaspoon garlic salt
½ chopped medium onion
¼ teaspoon salt
1 egg

DIRECTIONS

Combine all the ingredients and form small balls. Brown the meatballs in a skillet in Crisco oil and drain on paper towel. Bake, covered, for 30 minutes at 350 degrees. Immediately pour cream gravy over meatballs after removing from the oven.

INGREDIENTS FOR CREAM GRAVY

¼ cup bacon drippings
2 cups whole milk
⅓ cup flour
Salt and pepper to taste

DIRECTIONS

Heat bacon drippings in skillet, and sprinkle flour evenly into the drippings. Whisk until a golden brown paste is formed (a roux). If it's too greasy, add a bit more flour. Once golden, whisk in milk, stirring constantly. The gravy will thicken. If too thick, add a bit more milk. Season well with salt and pepper.

NOTE: Be sure to have your cream gravy on standby when you remove the meatballs from the oven.

Chef Hampton at your disposal. *Author Collection.*

BATHS

On Saturday nights, before plumbing, my family took baths in the kitchen, in turn, in a #3 washtub. When you get to Texas, ask your older audience if they ever heard about that #3 tub. They may begin to giggle.

Water was boiled on the stove in kettles and poured into the tub at temperatures rivaling a Louisiana crawfish cookout.

The youngest was first. My baby brother Dan, begging and pleading, was plunged into the caldron and scrubbed with bar soap and a "warsh rag." Dan had a ruddy complexion his whole life. I believe those baths had something to do with it. He was in and out pretty quickly so he could resume breathing. Then it was my turn.

Mama took special delight with me because I was always desperately in need of a bath. She said the same thing every Saturday night as she worked over my ears with a vengeance.

"There's enough dirt behind your ears to plant a row of corn!"

It is a phrase I will never forget. She probably didn't invent waterboarding, but she would approve of it. I know *I* would confess to anything in that steamy #3 washtub in the kitchen on Saturday night.

Last was my older brother Blake. By then the water was just right. He looked forward to that bath. Blake ended up being an artist and moved to Connecticut. Dan was a cowboy and a rodeo clown. He had a small ranch in Cushing, Oklahoma. I went to New York and Hollywood, where they paid you for having fun and making people laugh.

Me with my big brother Blake. *Author Collection.*

Me with my brothers Blake and Dan, a stack of Hamptons. *Author Collection.*

DAN

My brother Dan was quite a guy. He was a born animal trainer. He knew how to communicate with dogs, horses, and even goats. Dan was a *real* cowboy, and he picked one of the scariest jobs ever: rodeo clown.

When a bull rider is thrown from a bull, the only thing between him and a goring, trampling ton of meat is the rodeo clown. When he was a kid, Dan had a goat he had trained to butt him whenever he bent over. It was hilarious, and I guess it sort of prepared him for his future career.

Dan married a beautiful girl named Dixie and they had two children, Wick (named after Dan's hero, rodeo clown Wick Pith) and Missy. Dan's new father-in-law was very concerned about Dan's decision to continue rodeo clowning after he and Dixie were married and finally convinced him to try another career that wasn't so risky. With his father-in-law's recommendation, Dan went to work as a shoe salesman at a department store in downtown Fort Smith, Arkansas. He wasn't happy with the job, but everyone else breathed a sigh of relief.

Two weeks after he got the job, while transferring stock to the basement, Dan fell down an elevator shaft and broke his leg.

After he healed up, he went back to rodeo clowning. Being a shoe salesman was much too dangerous.

(Top) My brother Dan, aka "Horsefly." (Bottom) At the rodeo with Duke's Bob Harris, the voice of the Blue Devils. *Author Collection.*

TWO
CLASS CLOWN

I arrived at a tall registration desk to enroll at Crozier Tech High School and get my class schedules. I stood in line patiently. The lady there, the sign said she was Sadie Limmerhirt, kept taking the students in line behind me. After the third time, I realized she couldn't see me from her little cubicle because I was too short. At ninety-four pounds and just over five feet, I was the shortest boy in school. Naturally, I was embarrassed when the girl behind me patted me on the head, giggled, and went around me. That was it. I was done with high school. I didn't want to go anyway. It was my brother Blake's idea. He said I could learn a trade there. He eventually won a scholarship to Southern Methodist University because he was a talented artist and didn't need to learn a trade.

There was a pay phone in the hallway, so I dropped a nickel in and called Blake, who had graduated from Tech just a few months before. I was almost in tears and vowed not to enroll. He came to my rescue, as he had many times before and has since. He straightened things out. Ms. Limmerhirt allowed me to add choir and band to my curriculum. *Wait till they hear my soprano voice*, I thought. *At least I've got something going for me.*

Within a month my voice began to change. It sounded like I was yodeling, but not in a Roy Rogers kind of way. I made it through one semester in choir.

Never mind, I thought, *There's still the marching band with those beautiful majorettes.* I had played snare drum briefly in grade school, but the band teacher turned out to be a pedophile and he took off for Mexico and disappeared. We were allowed to pick an instrument that had been donated to the school. There was only one trumpet, which had seen better days, and a tenor saxophone. The sax looked impossible to play with all those buttons. I could get a sound out of the trumpet, and there were only three buttons. I wanted to play the trumpet like Harry James and then marry a girl like Betty Grable. I practiced hard for six weeks, but after the tryouts I was assigned to the percussion section.

Okay, I thought, *Maybe I can be another Gene Krupa.* Then a new guy joined the band and he really *could* play like Gene Krupa. He could play anything. He could play kettle drums, marimba, xylophone, and vibes. Colonel Crites, Tech's band teacher, handed me a pair of cymbals. Occasionally I would double on triangle. I could keep a good beat, though. The following year, I was promoted to bass drum. Finally, I thought I had found my niche. Four beats to a bar, accents on one and three. What could be simpler?

Strike Up the Band Egg and Sausage Casserole

INGREDIENTS

1 dozen eggs
1 cup grated cheddar cheese
1 small can of green chilis
1 pound ground sausage (Owens)
8 ounces of sour cream
Salt & pepper to taste
Fresh sliced mushrooms (Optional, but you don't know what you're missin' if you don't add 'em)

DIRECTIONS

Brown and drain sausage and set aside to cool. Mix together eggs, cheese, sour cream and green chilis, and add salt and pepper to taste. Mix in the cooked sausage. Pour mixture into a 9 x 13 casserole dish and bake at 350 degrees for 30 minutes. Serves 6-8.

It was the first football game of the season. We traveled in a special band bus to Corsicana, Texas. That was great because I had cousins I loved dearly who were in the Odd Fellows Widow's & Orphan's Home there, and I hoped that they could come see me play my big bass drum. We had been practicing for weeks. We made formations and we had some peppy songs to play. We were an ROTC band, so we wore military uniforms. Underneath it all, for added team spirit, I wore maroon boxer shorts with big white polka dots (our school colors). We had a special place to sit in the stands. It was all very exciting.

As you may not know, the most important person in a marching band is the drum major, followed by the bass drummer. This is how the beat is kept from one formation to another. In our case, we would march out to the field during halftime and spell out "WOLVES." Then we would break and run to the next formation and play another rousing song. Usually there would be three or four Sousa marches.

Every band member was responsible for their own instrument, except the heavy sousaphones (erroneously called tubas) and the big bass drum. We had the biggest bass drum in the city, and it had a picture of a snarling, angry wolf on one side. These instruments were brought in a separate van and placed in the stands.

The only thing I was obliged to bring was the chest harness, which supported the drum, and the beater. To my horror, those items had not made the trip. I was devastated. We assembled in the stands for our first number. The Crozier Tech fight song played as our team ran onto the field. I had a brainstorm. I took off my right penny loafer and began belting away. Boom, Boom, Boom. And nobody noticed. The only person who was looking my way was Colonel Crites, who was directing with his baton, while I was on the farthest bench away, dodging around behind the sousaphones. It looked like I was going to get away with it! I was so relieved that I began to relax and have a good time. That is, until we began to prepare for the halftime program. I had forgotten about that. I was a goner, doomed. How was I going to carry that big bass drum with one hand? If I couldn't make it work somehow, there would be no bass drum and, after all our hard work, no half-time show. Everyone would hate me. Again.

And then eureka! It came to me! I remembered a movie line that was used when things got tough: "You know, that's just crazy enough to work!"

First I undid my military web belt with the slide buckle. I skipped a belt loop and ran the six or seven inches of the belt through one of the drum tighteners near my middle, then I cinched it up as I tight as I could around my waist. I picked up the drum with my left hand by grabbing another tightener near my chin. My right hand held the loafer, and away we marched. At first, I didn't think anyone saw it. We went to our first position and played our fight song, and then we broke and ran to another formation. It was then that I noticed some people pointing curiously. The drum was heavy and my left arm was getting tired. I tried to lean back to help support the weight of the drum. It didn't help. I couldn't see over it, but I refused to give up and banged my shoe against the drum even harder.

One more formation to go. I staggered towards the final formation right in the middle of the field on the fifty-yard line. We were supposed to form a big "T." I started to run as best I could as the drum was beginning to bounce off the turf and I was bumping into trombones. I could feel my pants slipping. It was too late. The drum wasn't bouncing anymore: it had started to roll, and I was still attached. I rolled over the top of the drum, and then the drum rolled over the top of me, pulling my pants down around my knees.

By that time, both teams had returned to the field to see what was going on. I was trying to stand to pull up my pants. As luck would have it, my maroon-and-white polka-dot backside was facing our opponents. Everyone assumed I was part of the halftime show. When the Tech fans saw our colors, they rose to their feet and cheered. So, I gave a bow and waved. Colonel Crites was not amused. He banned me from riding back on the bus. Fortunately, my cousin Don was at the game and told me I could stay the night with him at the Odd Fellows Home. He was still laughing.

After that event, things changed for me. Classmates seemed to know my name. I received nods, waves, and smiles. I had become somebody. I remember an upperclassman who came over to me and said I should go see a movie with a guy "just like me" in it. He was referring to Jerry Lewis. I ran for sophomore class president and won. I was voted Class Wit in the yearbook. My "cred" was rising, but my grades were suffering. I was disruptive in classes and imitated teachers. I wasn't a bad kid, just one who craved attention.

Finally I was sent to the vice principal's office for the second time in a month. The last time, he had made me pick up wastepaper, gum wrappers, and any other trash around the school. Humiliating. Perry Fite was the most feared and revered person in school. He was a former

High school band camp stand up act. *Author Collection.*

football coach, a big tough individual with a no-nonsense personality. Once again, I stood before his desk. He ignored me completely. He seemed to be doodling on a piece of paper. After a while I cleared my throat. He looked up.

Mr. Fite: "What are you doing here?"

Me: "I was sent here."

I handed over a note from my commercial art teacher. Mr. Fite glanced at the note, wadded it up, and threw it into a waste can.

Mr. Fite: "Haven't you been here before?"

Me: "Yes, Sir."

Mr. Fite: "Didn't I tell you not to come back?"

I nodded. Mr. Fite folded up the folded paper he was doodling on and handed it to me.

Mr. Fite: "I don't have time for you. Take this over to the wood shop for me."

Me: "Yes, Sir!"

I couldn't believe my luck. All I had to do was run an errand for him. I took off like a shot. The shop teacher was the current baseball coach and very fit. I handed him the note and told me it was from Mr. Fite. He nodded and told me he would take care of it himself. He handed the note back to me and walked away. Several students were huddling, pointing, and smiling in my direction. I was curious, so I opened the note. It was a drawing of an enormous paddle, three inches wide, a half-inch thick, and a yard long! It had a handle cut in one end. The thing looked like a cricket bat. I tried to look nonchalant. The coach returned with the bat and a half dozen interested

shop guys following behind.

The coach said, "You know, we have a credo here. Nothing leaves this shop without being tested. We are proud of what we make here. So, bend over and grab your ankles."

Oh no.

He took a swing like Joe DiMaggio. It lifted me out of my crouched position and up in the air. I realized I had not stopped breathing, but I could only take short gasps. My eyes watered and my nose ran, but I didn't cry. I couldn't, to tell the truth. From far way, I heard a bell ring. It was the end of the period.

"Well son, it looks like this is as good a paddle as we have ever made," the coach muttered.

There were murmurs of agreement. It was a good one all right. The coach handed it over and I limped away. *All in all*, I thought, *I would rather be picking up gum wrappers.*

I walked down the long hall and entered Mr. Fite's outer office where a pretty girl was typing. She looked at me with compassion as I went into Mr. Fite's office. Once more I was ignored. Finally, he looked up.

Mr. Fite: "What do you want?"

Me: "You sent me to get this paddle made."

Mr. Fite: "Oh, I don't have time for that. Paddle yourself."

Me: (Total disbelief) "Sir?"

Mr. Fite: "Stand over there and paddle yourself."

I obediently went to the spot he indicated and began to paddle tentatively. I was still sore from the smack on the rear from the coach.

Mr. Fite: "If you want me to show you how that's done . . ."

Me: "Oh, no sir! I'm getting the hang of it."

I began to whack away for about ten minutes while Mr. Fite paid no attention. I decided to try once more.

Me: "Mr. Fite?"

Mr. Fite: (Disgruntled) "What is it now?"

Me: "How long do I have to do this?"

Mr. Fite: "Until you're through."

Me: "Well, I'm pretty sure my bottom is red."

Mr. Fite: "Drop your pants and let me see."

At that precise moment the pretty girl in the front office leaned around the corner.

Me: "Never mind, sir. I was just kidding."

I went back to paddling, Mr. Fite went back to doodling, and the pretty girl went back to typing until the last bell rang. I walked over to Mr. Fite and placed the paddle on his desk. He looked me directly in the eye.

Mr. Fite: "Have you learned anything?"

Me: "Yes, Sir, I have. I learned that because of my actions, I'm the one who is hurting me."

Mr. Fite: "Bingo! Here, (handing me the paddle) throw this in the trash. We won't need this anymore."

From that moment everything changed. I went from a "C" average to a member of the National Honor Society. I was elected as class president twice, sergeant at arms in the student government, cheerleader, treasurer at Texas Boys State in Austin, and was offered a scholarship from the Harvard Club in Dallas (which, unfortunately, I was unable to accept because of monetary requirements that had to be met by my parents who always seemed to be struggling financially).

Mr. Fite encouraged me to do a lip sync of "What it Was, Was Football" by Andy Griffith for the football banquet. The phonograph conked out, but I did it anyway. It was my first "stand-up." It got laughs.

I'll always owe you one, Mr. Fite.

My very best friend Jim Bob Baugh and I loved the fair. The State Fair of Texas was a respite from school, and in fact, there is one day every October that schools in Dallas close in order for kids to attend the fair. This day pointed the way for my future career as an actor.

Jim Bob and I liked to get there early. When I say early, I mean the minute it opened. Once we were through the turnstiles we took off for the midway. That's where all the action was—the rides, the food, the hoochie-coochie dancers, and the possibility of winning some treasure you could give to your mom. We were trying to decide what we were going to eat, corny dogs or funnel cakes, when a guy who ran the dart-throw booth called us over. He asked us if we wanted to make a little money. We were indeed interested.

He took us around behind his booth. It was completely different from what could be seen from the front. There were trailers and people bustling about, getting ready for the day and night shows. Then, the Dart Man showed us the back of the dartboards. There were four of them, about five feet wide and four feet high, made of some sort of porous white substance. The boards were on swivels, front

(Left) How'd I not make the team? (Right) Yell Leader at Crozier Tech High. *Author Collection.*

My high school graduation photo. *Author Collection.*

A bunch of jailbirds at the State Fair of Texas. *Author Collection.*

and back. From the front, it was a sea of small balloons, from the back, it was littered with burst balloons hanging forlornly from thumbtacks, victims of accurate darts.

Next, we were shown how to use an air tank to blow up a balloon to the size of a grapefruit. It only took a few seconds for the Dart Man to blow up a balloon, tie it off, and replace it. He was a master. When the balloons were getting sparse, on a signal from the front, the board would be spun around and ready for more suckers. That's what I said. Just take my word for it. If you did break some balloons, you received coupons that could be redeemed for prizes from the lower shelves. The carnies called the lower-shelf prizes "trash" and the higher shelves "flash." The Dart Man was called Sid and he paid us well at fifty cents an hour, every hour.

Sid had a partner named Sonny who came in later to give us a break. He was faster at blowing up balloons than both of us put together and managed to keep a Lucky Strike lit to boot. We were glad he showed up because Jim Bob and I were hungry. We had corny dogs and root beer. We decided to go tell Sid we were moving on from the carney life and had a plan to go ride the bumper cars. Sid smiled and paid us six quarters each. As we were leaving he called me over. He spoke quietly.

Sid: "How old are you Jimmy?" I was fourteen but looked more like ten.

Me: "Sixteen."

Sid: "How would you like to make five bucks?"

I yelled at Jim Bob that I would catch up to him later.

Me: "What you got in mind?"

Sid: "I want you to take that big panda bear off the top shelf."

Me: "Sure."

Sid: "Then I want you to walk up and down the midway for an hour or so."

Me: "I don't get it."

Sid: "You will. Before you know it, a big ol' boy will come over to you with a pretty girl hanging on his arm and he's going to say to you, 'Say kid, where did you get that big panda bear?' And you say, 'Over at the Dart Throw! Three for a quarter!' Do you think you can do that, Jim?"

Me: "Yes, Sir!"

Sid: "I knew you were one of us. Here's a five-dollar bill. I'm paying you now. It may get a little crowded over here later on."

And it happened just like that, right down to big ol' boys with pretty girls on their arms. All of them wanted

11

to know where I got that big panda bear. I even ad-libbed a line at the end: "It's real easy!"

I know it was the State Fair of Texas midway and not Broadway, but it was acting, and I got paid for it. Oh, and people want to know what the trick was to winning that big panda. I can't tell you that because I'm still a carney at heart. But I will say this: the Dart Throw is more on the level than trying to knock down milk bottles with a baseball.

My best pals, Jim Bob Baugh and Bob Porter. *Author Collection.*

THREE
COLLEGE DAYS

Me as Benedick in the NTSC production of *Much Ado About Nothing*. *Author Collection.*

You are probably wondering what all this has to do with becoming an actor. It is my contention that everything has to do with that very thing. I promise I'll be as brief as I can.

Now, where were we? Oh yes, college.

My freshman year at North Texas State College (now the University of North Texas) in Denton was illuminating. I thought I wanted to be an artist. My older brother, Blake, was an outstanding artist and illustrator, and as a child I wanted to be just like him. I copied everything he did. I worked on the techniques he used. I took commercial art classes for four years at Crozier Tech High School, where Blake had preceded me, and I was pretty darn good. Although I was one of the best student-artists in the school, after I really thought about it, I knew I could never be the best artist in my own family! I could

draw anything I was looking at, but Blake could draw, paint, or sketch anything he'd ever seen or imagined. It was time for me to have a talk with myself. I needed to change my major.

It was around this time that I saw Pat Boone doing a Greek tragedy. I think he was Orestes. He was very good. We became friends and pledged the same fraternity that year, Kappa Alpha. I took Pat to Curry's Collegiate Shop, where I insisted he buy his first pair of white bucks. Pat, Shirley, and I have, to this day, remained the closest of friends.

I'm pretty ashamed to admit why I changed my major from art to speech and drama. I wish I could say that acting had always been in my blood, that I wanted to perform in great plays, or even that I had a need to perform. Some of that is partially true, but honestly I think I did it because the girls in speech and drama were really cute, especially one Miss Marilyn Agan. She was a knockout.

Mind you, there were some great-looking women in the music department, but as you recall, I have zero musical talent. The thing that tipped the scales was the ratio. There were about three females to one male. If only I could have been a dancer. Unfortunately, that would require a sense of rhythm and balance. I had neither. What I did have is a desire for fame and a thirst for laughter and applause. The first play I was cast for was *The Insect Comedy*. I played the Ichneumon Fly.

I plugged along learning everything I could. I was a good scenery painter, and my buddy Robert Baruch could

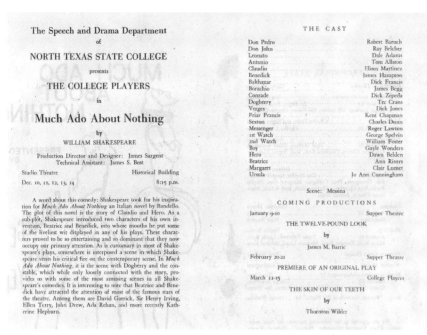

Playbill from the NTSC production of *Much Ado About Nothing*.
Author Collection.

RST ROW: McCune, Creswell, Maberry, Officer, Knight, Barker, Woodruff, Hansen, Stearns. SECOND ROW: Shepherd, Ellsworth, McNamara, roadfoot, Fitzpatrick, Dugan, Rollins, Bayard, Starks, Baden. THIRD ROW: King, McCarley, Hampton, McKee, Manning, Kaufhold, Webb, Illiams.

College Players Begin "Earn Membership" Plan

College Players this year initiated an "earn your membership" plan. Prospective thespians assisted with make-up, props, scenery, and lighting work, or appeared in productions. The apprenticeship time requirement was 25 hours.

The busy dramatists presented six plays during '55-'56 season, opening with "Dial M for Murer." Other productions were "Arms and the Man,"

"The Private Lives of the Master Race," "Ways and Means," and "The Theatre of the Soul." During the Fine Arts the group presented "Macbeth."

Also new to the Players this year was a laboratory theatre. Students alternated at projects of directing, acting, and working at other phases of play production. Lab members presented their projects before meetings of the group.

The college players at NTSC for the '55 – '56 season. *Author Collection.*

build anything. Bob had a great attitude, and he told me every year that we would get good parts. This from a guy who played the Dung Beetle. I was Eeyore, and he was right. We hit the jackpot: *Much Ado About Nothing* by Shakespeare. Bob wanted to be Dogberry, and I was lucky enough to snag the role of Benedick. I did as much research as I could in the library. I found out what the jokes were about, and it paid off. Some of the references were a bit risqué. Once I discovered this information, the audience seemed to catch on. I learned that Shakespeare could be quite a funny guy.

The College Players also did a one-act antiwar play by Edna St. Vincent Millay called *Aria da Capo*, an amazing verse play in which two shepherds become so involved in a silly game that they kill each other. I learned that Millay was an extremely thought-provoking lady.

When I had spare time, I spent it in the library or in the auditorium. The auditorium was used on a daily basis by students who played the massive pipe organ or those rehearsing an opera. It was here that I first became aware of an opera teacher named Mary McCormic.

This lady was already a legend. She was rumored to be an Italian princess, via an ex-prince, ex-husband who gave her a palazzo in Venice. She directed from the audience while smoking from a long cigarette holder, and she could hit a high C at will. We became friends. More about her later, but I will say she had a major role in how I got started in show business. I tried to tell you this is the long version. We are about halfway, I think.

My senior year was a bit rocky. I ran out of money. So I joined the Naval Air Reserve, and I became a Navy petty officer third class recruit trainer in boot camp. I sent all my checks home to be deposited in the bank. However, when I tried to enroll for my final semester, the check bounced. I had no money. My mom had "borrowed" it thinking she could repay it, but she wasn't able to. I was broke. This meant no tuition. Consequently, I never finished college, although my alma

The wonderful Mary McCormic.
Author Collection.

mater saw fit to deem me Alumnus of the Year in 1981, of which I am most proud. I still root for the Eagles and, as a former cheerleader, get in free to the games. I like free.

My wife likes scary stuff. She asked me once if I ever had a "paranormal experience." I told her I had once, while in college. Sort of. Rapt with attention, she pressed me for the story. Here it is.

After an evening of cruising for girls and over-indulging in Pabst Blue Ribbon, my pal Bob Porter and I were driving by the Denton police station in his snazzy convertible when a genius idea struck me. *Hey! Wouldn't it be funny to throw empty beer cans at that building?* I stood up and proceeded to do just that very thing. A few minutes later, Bob was pulled over. Apparently, the Denton cops didn't share my can-throwing enthusiasm. Being the true friend that he was, Bob, who was slightly less inebriated than I, promptly confessed to the crime. No go. He had a kind face. I had a guilty looking one. I was immediately brought before the chief.

Chief: "Hampton, how much money do you have on you?"

Me: "A dollar forty, Sir."

Chief: "Hand it over. That's part of your fine. You're going to have to do some community service."

Me: "Yes, Sir."

Chief: "You've got mowing detail at the Denton cemetery. Twenty hours."

Me: "Starting when?"

Chief: "Tomorrow."

While I appreciated the fact that I had gotten off light, I was not overly excited about my friends and fraternity brothers seeing me mow the cemetery lawn. So, I had another genius idea. I'd mow it under the cover of darkness. At night, when no one would know. Brilliant!

The next evening, around midnight, I was at the cemetery with my push mower. I was about half an hour into my chore when the lights of a squad car approached. Two cops got out and began walking over. Cop Number One shined his flashlight on me.

Cop Number One: "Hampton, is that you?"

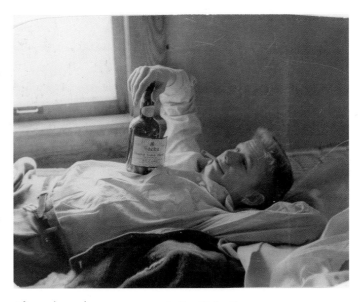

After a long day on campus. *Author Collection.*

15

Me: "Yes, Sir."

Cop Number One: "What are you doing out here this time of night?"

Me: "My community service, Sir."

Silence. Then peals of laughter from the two cops.

Cop Number One: "Get outta here, Hampton."

Apparently, a woman who lived across the street from the cemetery had called the Denton police. She was hysterical. When asked what she wanted to report she told them, "There's a ghost in the cemetery and you'll never believe what it's doing!"

I never did finish my community service. Sorry Denton. I still owe you nineteen and a half hours.

During school I had worked for a photographer in Denton, but he couldn't afford to hire me either. The economy was not doing well. I got a job with UPI in Dallas, but the pay was low. I worked as an assistant director and met a young Brenda Vaccaro whose father, Mario, gave me a job at his Italian restaurant parking cars and mixing drinks. He was a wonderful man who showed me how to work in a restaurant, which many actors have found necessary before their big break. I worked for a while at two other restaurants, saved my tips, and in the fall of 1958, I headed for New York City and Broadway. I was getting to be more of a Pooh than an Eeyore.

(Top) Stand Up Act at NTSC with Pal Neal Weaver. (Bottom Left) My boy flat top. (Bottom Right) Father Time, New Year's 1957. *Author Collection.*

FOUR
NEW YORK: TAKE ONE

If you have a bucket list of things to do or see before you croak, make sure you plan to see the Big Apple in the fall. I arrived in Manhattan in mid-October. It was more than beautiful. My brother Blake let me sleep on his couch until I could get a job and get settled. I would also babysit their beautiful baby daughter, Caroline, on occasion. They lived in a lovely apartment on the Upper East Side between Lexington and Third Avenues. Central Park was a short walk away, and buses and subways were nearby as well. I was ecstatic. My favorite hangouts were the Metropolitan Museum and an Irish pub a half a block from the apartment. There was only one thing missing: I had no plan as to how I was going to become an actor. I had a lot of jobs, but none had anything to do with acting. A fellow has to eat, you know.

Tree lounging in New York. *Author Collection.*

Still horsing around with Pat Boone. *Author Collection.*

JOB NO. 1: JEWELRY GOON

Pat Boone was hot in those days. I mean Elvis hot. Pat, Shirley, a few friends, and I were dining out one evening when Pat greeted a gregarious fellow and asked him to join us. His name was George Unger, and he was a jeweler. He sold jewelry to people like Pat, Harry Belafonte, and of course, Sammy Davis Jr. It turned out that George carried his entire line of merchandise in a leather briefcase. In the course of the evening, he decided I would make an ideal bodyguard. When I asked what my duties were, he told me to guard the merchandise.

"What if somebody with a gun wants the merchandise?" I asked.

"Give it to them for God's sake. What, are you crazy? I'm insured."

I took the job.

JOB NO. 2: BABYSITTER TO THE STARS

I ran into a friend from Dallas who, along with another guy, was looking for a third roommate to share expenses. So I moved from my brother's couch to theirs. We lived across the street from the wonderful Ansonia Hotel. Many voice teachers still coach some of the most famous singers in the world there. To walk down Seventy-Third Street and hear such beautiful music pouring out of the open windows makes you feel all is right with the world.

The only problem was that I was running out of money again. George Unger was a wonderful man, but he often forgot to pay me. When I did get "paid," George would take off his gold watch or a ring and hand it to me. Of course, I couldn't accept them.

George also volunteered me for jobs with celebrity friends that didn't pay much if anything at all. For instance, I babysat for Harry Belafonte and his wife once. Mr. B was generous and gave me two tickets to his show at the Waldorf Astoria. That was terrific, but I needed some dough.

It didn't take me long to learn that when celebrities do try to pay you, they seldom have a bill smaller than a C-note, so that made for a few awkward moments.

It was time to look for something else.

JOB NO. 3: TOY MAN

I became a toy demonstrator. It was for a hockey game sold by Abraham & Straus in Brooklyn, New York. The game box was about thirty-six by eighteen inches and looked like a tiny ice-hockey rink. If you have ever seen a foosball setup, they are similar. There are levers that slide the "men" back and forth and spin around when they are in position for a shot on goal or a pass to another teammate. I got very good at playing the game. I didn't have to think about what I was doing, and operating the men happened with ease. I could play with one hand and still win. I didn't sell any, though. I thought maybe it was a little pricey at $11.99. What was I doing wrong? I had plenty of shoppers watching me play like Bobby Orr. They were lined up to play me, but when I tried to actually close the deal they began to wander off. I took a break.

I was approached by a middle-aged, well-dressed man who offered to buy me a drink. I needed one. We went to a bar across the street. The bartender seemed to know him, and the man ordered two Depth Bombs. I had never heard of such a drink. The bartender set up two glasses of beer and two jiggers of rye. The man told me his name was Ray as he dropped the jiggers of rye, shot glasses and all, into our glasses of beer.

He said, "Here's how," and we chugged the concoctions. "You want to know why nobody is buying your toy, right?"

I nodded.

He continued, "It's because you win every time. It looks too hard, takes all the fun out of it. In Brooklyn we like to win once in a while."

He gave me a big wink and walked away from the bar, leaving a five-dollar bill as we headed back to A&S.

"Let's have some fun while we test my theory, Jim. When I pull on my right ear, you tank, but you got to sell it like you was trying real hard, you know . . . act!"

Act? He had found my weak spot. That afternoon I sold four hockey games. By the end of the week, I had done well. So did Ray. Turned out he was a bookie.

Merry Christmas.

JOB NO. 4: PRESERVING THE ARTS

Christmas passed, and I was going broke again. I applied through an employment agency which found me a job working in a photo lab. The photo company had been commissioned to photograph all American art. It would take years, but I was desperate for immediate funds, and I thought I could continue my quest once I got on my feet. The job paid $53.82, after taxes. That sounded like a lot of money. I signed on the dotted line. The downside was that the employment agency took the first week's wages as their cut of the pie. I had less than ten dollars left to last a week in New York City, which included getting back and forth to work (thirty cents each way on the subway) and food expenses. I had a few ideas.

For breakfast I would have a coffee and a Danish at a deli around the corner; cost: twenty cents. Lunch was a hot dog with sauerkraut (don't forget your vegetables) and a soda from a pushcart on the steps of the New York Library, a block and a half from work; cost: fifteen cents. An afternoon snack could be had at the Automat. For a dime, you received a cup, saucer, and a tea bag. You carried these items on a tray to a service area where there was an electric carafe for your tea, silverware, glasses, napkins, ice, crackers, and condiments. Here's the drill: You place your cup with the tea bag under the spout and fill it with hot water. You place the saucer on top of the cup in order to accelerate the steeping of the tea. Meanwhile, place butter on the saucer to soften. You fill an empty glass with ice, sugar, and squeezed lemon to taste. Empty the tea into the ice-filled glass and fill the cup with hot water and catsup. Voila! Tomato soup with buttered crackers and iced tea. Repeat if necessary. Dinner: about twenty-five cents at McSorley's, and it included two glasses of ale and a sandwich with the occasional pickled hardboiled egg. Total daily expenditure: seventy cents, more or less.

Everything was looking up. I liked my boss and my coworkers. A friend from Texas offered me keys to his apartment since he was going to Buenos Aires. All I had to do was make the monthly rent of twenty-six dollars. So I moved my meager belongings into a three-room apartment on Hester Street, between Mott and Mulberry. I was all set. I felt like an official New Yorker. Broadway, here I come!

Just one thing: on April 1, 1959, I was drafted in the army.

FIVE
MILITARY MAN

Four Swabbies, 1958. *Author Collection.*

Private Hampton, US Army. *Author Collection.*

The army? How could that happen? I was a petty officer third class in the United States Naval Air Force Reserve. There were additional complications, not the least of which was that it was April Fool's Day, and no one would believe me. My brother Blake finally let it sink in and said he would see what he could do. I took the subway, ran from the stop to my job, and explained to my boss that it wasn't a prank and that at that very moment, I was technically AWOL. He wrote out a check, handed it over, and wished me luck. I barely made the bus.

Next stop: Fort Dix, New Jersey. Not counting the driver, I was the oldest one on the bus. It wasn't a long trip, but I did learn that the F word could be used as a verb, noun, *and* adverb. A sentence was conjured up by a draftee before the day was done.

"F you, you F-ing F!"

It sounded like the cast of the *Sopranos*.

After dinner we were given ill-fitting fatigues and

boots. I didn't think it could get worse until it started raining. The United States Army didn't seem to notice. I was picked by one of the three-stripers to wash the pots and pans . . . outside . . . in the rain. We were given a pillow, a pillowcase, a blanket, and a sheet. I was bone tired. *Maybe tomorrow we'll get sorted out*, I thought. I slept almost immediately.

The next morning reveille was sounded, and we hurriedly dressed and went to breakfast. It was a vile concoction of canned beef and gravy slopped on toast. Afterward we assembled on the parade ground. The top sergeant looked pissed off as he tried to read a memo. He cleared his throat.

"Is there a John Hampton here?"

At first I missed it. Then I wondered if maybe he was talking about me. I raised my hand tentatively and tried to sound as military as I could.

"Could it be *James* Hampton, Sergeant?"

He looked at his note and gestured at me to follow

him. I did so. He wasn't exactly chatty, but he asked if I had eaten. I nodded my head.

We entered one of the plain buildings with lots of offices and passed a lot of noncoms typing and cleaning. One spec four who was typing looked familiar. I thought I was delusional. He was the image of Pat Boone's brother, Nick. We were met by a major who was nice enough to ask if I had eaten. I told him I hadn't, and he shot a look at the sergeant major, who saluted and left. I followed the major to a large office where a bird colonel was holding a phone and indicated it was for me. It was the general of Fort Dix on the line.

Uh oh, I thought. *I'm in trouble already. Maybe I didn't clean the pots and pans good enough when I was on K.P. last night. Maybe I'm not in the army after all and this is all a nightmare. Maybe I should take this call. It's a general. Must be important!*

General: "Is this Private James Hampton?"

Me: "I guess so, Sir. Except maybe for the 'private' part."

General: "Have you had chow?"

Me: "Yes, Sir. Thank you, Sir, general, Sir."

General: "What was on the menu?"

Me: "Well, in the navy, Sir, it's called 'SOS.'"

General: (laughing) "We call it that in the army too, Son. Lyndon Johnson's office called late yesterday. Your brother said you were 'kidnapped by the army.' We thought it was someone playing a joke. It wasn't. Some of my staff was up quite late trying to sort this out. Apparently, your papers were lost somewhere between Dallas and New Orleans."

Me: "What does that mean to me, Sir?"

General: "Your draft board created a big snafu."

Me: "We say that in the navy too, Sir."

General: "You're in the army now, Son. Even though your draft board made a mistake, the army takes precedent because you're now on active duty and not in the reserve. You'll be discharged from the navy reserve at some future date, but it won't interfere with your duties in the army. You'll take part in basic training, et cetera, until your two-year obligation to the army is satisfied."

Me: "What do you recommend, Sir?"

General: "Just try to make the best of it. I must say you are taking this well. May I tell Lyndon Johnson's office that you're happy?"

Me: "I don't think I'd go that far, Sir. How about 'patriotic'?"

General: "You got it. If there's anything I can do . . . "

Me: "Well, I always wanted to go to Europe, Sir."

General: "Done! I'll notify LBJ that you are patriotic."

Kidnapped by the army, 1959. *Author Collection.*

Me: "Thank you, Sir."

On my way out I saw that the guy typing was indeed Pat Boone's brother Nick. Somehow, I took that as a good sign. I felt better right away.

Nick whispered, "How did it go in there, Jim?"

"Aw, you know me," I said. "Generals are putty in my hands."

Nick gave me the thumbs-up sign, then mouthed, "Four more months and out for me!"

The general was as good as his word. In a couple of weeks my entire regiment was transferred to Fort Knox, Kentucky, to begin training for Bavaria. When we arrived at Fort Knox, I was assigned to . . . F Troop Sixth Armored Cavalry.

Coincidence? Hmmmm. We'll see.

Fort Knox, Kentucky, in the summertime is tougher than a boot. Maybe that's why they call it boot camp. In

"I'm in the Navy, Uh, Army Now" Bean Soup

Oh, if only the food had been this good!!!

INGREDIENTS

1 pound navy beans (pick out the rocks)
1 pound bone-in ham
1 large baking potato, peeled and quartered
½ cup milk
2 tablespoons butter
1 large onion, chopped fine
1 stalk celery, small dice
2 cloves garlic, chopped fine
¼ cup parsley, chopped
Salt and pepper to taste

DIRECTIONS

Soak beans overnight in cold water in a large covered bowl. They will swell. Drain the beans and place them in a large pot. Add 10 cups of water and the ham. Bring to a simmer over medium heat, then reduce to low and cook until the beans are tender. Remove the ham and set aside to cool. Remove the bone, dice the ham, and return to the pot. Boil the potato in salted water until tender, but not falling apart. Drain, and mash the potato with milk until smooth. Add the mash to the bean soup and stir until combined. Melt the butter in a skillet and sauté onion, celery, garlic, and parsley until all vegetables are translucent (about 10 minutes). Add the vegetable mixture to the bean soup. Cook on low for 60 minutes, adding up to 2 additional cups of water to prevent over-thickening. Season with salt and pepper.

Sop* it up with a good piece of cornbread!

*Just in case you don't know: "Sop" (verb)—To Soak up liquid using an absorbent substance.

---

any case, it was good for me physically. I aced all the tests because I had already taken them in the navy. I even once taught the Uniform Code of Military Justice to the "boots."

I remembered the general's advice to "make the best of it." He didn't say I couldn't have a little amusement.

First, there was "fun" with inspections. Inspections encompass multiple tasks:

1. The barracks: our sleeping area and our toilet should be spotless.

2. Our cots: blankets and sheets are tight enough to bounce a quarter on them.

3. Our fatigue uniforms: washed and ironed, all brass polished, with special attention to boots and buckles.

4. Inspection of our metal lockers and footlockers: only certain things could be inside of the lockers, and everything had to be arranged carefully. In our footlockers, we had a shaving kit containing tooth powder, Sutton Stick (underarm deodorant), razor, and soap. We were allowed two books: the Bible and a book of our choosing.

Here is where the fun began. The book of my choosing was *The Myth of Sisyphus* by Albert Camus. The platoon leader glanced at our company commander, Captain Tom Kelly, who was trying hard not to smile. He picked up the book and looked me in the eyes.

Captain Kelly: "Don't you know that Camus is a French atheist? Have you read this book?"

Me: "Sir, yes, Sir."

Captain Kelly: "What did you learn?"

Me: "That repeating the same actions over and over and expecting different results is insane, Sir."

The second lieutenant's face was getting red and the captain wasn't too sure whether or not Private Hampton was on the level. He continued to stare at me as he opened my metal upright locker. Instead of a photo on the door, where most guys have a picture of their sweetheart, there was picture of Lyndon Baines Johnson descending a ramp at Love Field in Dallas, Texas. Behind him, his attractive daughter Lynda Bird Johnson was waving and smiling.

Written on the picture in a woman's hand was: "Dear Jimmy, I miss you. Come home soon. Love, Lynda B."

Captain Kelly: "Carry on, Private."

That picture was in my locker for my entire military career. Thanks to Bob Porter, my roommate at NTSC, who got the photo on assignment at the *Dallas Times Herald*, and Pat Porter, his lovely wife, who had signed it. Due to their brilliance, I never had a problem during any inspection. In fact, I sort of enjoyed them.

I didn't enjoy advanced infantry training. There was a

place there called Misery Hill. Part of our training included marching up the hill with a full pack, carrying an M1 infantry rifle. I also carried our stanchion. It was a struggle. Halfway up the hill, Captain Kelly reached over, took my backpack, and strapped it on his own back. Years later, we all watched General Tom Kelly on the nightly news as he explained to us what was going on in the Gulf War. Not too bad for a guy who was trained in the ROTC.

I will never forget his kindness and sense of humor, or his relieving me of my backpack on a boiling-hot summer day in Kentucky. A few weeks later, we were on a military transport plane for a long flight to Frankfurt, Germany. From there, we were separated and scattered across Germany. I was attached to another outfit in the beautiful city of Regensburg. Headquarters was in Straubing, right smack on the Danube. Our colonel was the son of General George Patton. Soon we were preparing for war games and Operation Winter Shield.

As winter came and snow began to fall, I thought it would be fun. As a kid I loved playing war games. I had never tried them in the winter. We were welcomed with a blizzard and a hard freeze. A few guys lost their lives due to accidents or simply not following orders. I started to think about the summer in Fort Knox. The army prepared us for extremes, I guessed. In any case, we learned how to pack up and go anywhere in a short time. My unit's time had come. We were to relieve another outfit on the Czech border.

We grabbed our gear and set out. I felt like a real soldier, but the soldiers we were relieving were the real thing. They had endured and completed their assignment. My helmet was off to them. We were apprehensive newcomers. We learned that some men had psychological problems. The assignments were twenty-four hours on and twenty-four hours off. There was precious little to do during the off time except drink and try to sleep. The USO didn't come that far. A small tavern provided the local brew. That was pretty much it, not very heroic. Some guys flipped out. We were told one story about a soldier cutting himself up with a razor in order to be sent home. My buddies and I decided they were pulling our legs, but we were going to be careful nonetheless.

Our first trip to the border was sobering. We were separated from a possible enemy by fifty yards of plowed ground. Our orders were to observe them, but not to engage them. Similar orders were issued for Sitting Bull and the Sioux. First, we took inventory.

1. Manpower: them, 150 to 200 men; us, six

Me and Bob Porter with matching flat tops. *Author Collection.*

2. Motor equipment: them, fifty tanks; us, two jeeps
3. Armament: them, fifty tanks; us, one thirty-caliber machine gun, six rifles, and one Bazooka

All jokes aside, it was a little daunting. We took turns watching the guard on a wooden tower fifty yards away. We were in a concrete bunker with the machine gun pointed at one of their tower guards. Our orders were to notate in a log what the guard did and when he did it, including when he urinated off the tower. I wondered if he had similar orders.

I admit I was feeling a little low, tired, and sleepy that Christmas of 1959. I told my spec-four that I needed a break. It was granted, and I wandered off into the Black Forest. The snow was knee deep and the silence overwhelming. In my thoughts, I cried out to God, *Lord, is this the best we can do? Is mankind unable to settle differences without murdering each other? Got a better idea?* The following thoughts came in the form of an internal dialogue.

God: *Have you done your best?*
Me: *What do you mean?*
God: *What do you want to be?*

Me: *I've always dreamed of becoming an actor.*

God: *Have you done your best to become one?*

Me: *I guess not.*

God: *Why not?*

Me: *Because I'm afraid.*

God: *What are you afraid of?*

Me: *If I try as hard as I can, and I fail, I won't even have a dream.*

God: *But, don't you see that if you don't try, you will never reach your goal?*

Me: *I hadn't thought of it like that. Okay, as soon as I can get out of the army, I'll try as hard as I can to become an actor!*

God: *Oh, no. You don't understand. You can have the day off because it's Christmas, but then you have to start.*

Me: *But how can I do that? I'm in the army with bullets and stuff.*

God: *You just let me handle the details.*

And that was that. The next day I was summoned by the top sergeant. Headquarters in Straubing had ordered me to three days of temporary duty. I was to operate a spotlight for a colonel who was going back to the United States. I never went back to that cold Czech border. My stuff was sent to me. I went to work in Special Services, but that is another story.

Just kidding. This is the long version of the question, "How did I get started?"

I ran the spotlight for the colonel's party, and I emceed the evening as well. I turned it into a roast, and thank God the colonel had a sense of humor. When folks in the military have a few days off before they go home, everybody kids them about how short they are getting.

I said, "The colonel is so short he could play handball on a curb!"

Junior officers in attendance got into the spirit (as well as the "spirits") and passed the microphone around. The evening was a huge success. All the brass shook my hand and the incoming colonel was a great guy.

After the roast, I learned how I got there. It was the Civilian Special Services coordinator, Harry Murray. We got along from the start because I was from Texas and he from Arkansas. According to him, he was looking through files for somebody who could run a spotlight. Since my college major was theater arts, he thought I ought to be able to do it. It wasn't too tough—plug it in and turn it on. Harry needed an assistant, and he was a genius at sidestepping red tape. I was added to the special services roster and was able to fill in in several areas. I accompanied USO shows to the border where the men

Stand up act in the army. *Author Collection.*

needed it most, did stand-up comedy, and stayed out of trouble. I was given a desk along with a Czech secretary (I guess she crossed the border at night) who spoke three languages, and a sergeant who ran the movie theater. His motto seemed to be, "Never rock the boat." I tried to be invisible when war games were played, wore civvies, and drove a VW van. The motor pool didn't miss it, according to Harry.

I was billeted with the MPs and the band. We had a blast. To this day, I couldn't tell you who's more fun to hang with, cops or musicians.

After a few months, Harry's contract expired and all of us, including our female librarians Pat, Donna, and Connie, threw a dinner for him. We all got pissed on Bavarian beer out of a gigantic stein. Harry was taking a 10:00 p.m. train to Munich and catching a flight from there. We all staggered into the train station with little time to spare. The girls were crying, and the men were weaving unsteadily. As the train was pulling out of the station, I jumped on the back of it, gave Harry a big smooch, jumped back onto the platform, and waved

Bavarian holiday in the army. *Author Collection.*

With the cast of *The Tender Trap* with Herb Wills, Straubing.
Author Collection.

Esther Williams presents an individual SACom award to Jim Hampton, star and director of "The Tender Trap," the play presented by the Straubing Community Theater which will represent SACom in the forthcoming 1960 USAREUR Tournament of Plays. Miss Williams made this and other individual presentations at the Dachau Service Club last Sunday. In the background is Lt Col James F. Sullivan, SACom Special Services Officer.

US ARMY PHOTO BY HALLOWELL

Area Winners in Play Tourney Awarded By Esther Williams

MUNICH—Following a performance of the SACom Tournament of Plays prize-winning play, "The Tender Trap," Sunday evening, 20 Nov, at the Dachau Service Club, actress Esther Williams presented the cast and back stage crew with trophies.

Besides presenting the individual awards, Miss Williams also presented Jim Hampton, star and director of the play, with the SACom trophy. A special presentation was also made by Miss Williams to Harry Murray,

Straubing Entertainment Director, for his work during his stay in Straubing. Mr Murray will be leaving for the US in the near future.

Miss Donna Cloud was presented a silver plaque by Miss Williams for being selected as the SACom Actress of the Year.

Following the presentation there was a buffet dinner, at which time Miss Williams posed for pictures.

Miss Williams is in Munich for the filming of her next motion picture.

Receiving SACom Award from Esther Williams. *Author Collection.*

my hanky. Harry's expression was worth all the beer in Bavaria. I had a hangover for three days.

When the fog cleared, I cleaned out Harry's desk because we were adding a travel bureau, and we needed the space. Much to my surprise, I came across several plays. They were published by Samuel French. One of the plays was called *The Tender Trap*. I remembered a movie by that title starring Frank Sinatra, so I read the play that day. I knew immediately that we had to do it. It was equally funny for men and women. I spread the word and put sign-up sheets everywhere. The officers' wives had a club that totally backed us. Everyone got excited about the *Trap*. We had the best group of people I have ever worked with. Everyone was wonderful, both onstage

and off.

All our hard work that summer paid off. *The Tender Trap* was a huge hit and a morale booster. Our colonel wrote us letters of commendation. We even won awards. I ended up with a silver tray as Best Actor—European Command. I received my silver platter from Esther Williams, who gave me a big kiss! An audience of GIs went berserk. My heart was pounding so hard it could have been heard in the fifth row. I was invited to perform a Moss Hart play in Munich titled *Light Up the Sky*, and if that wasn't enough, when I got back to Straubing, I received my honorable discharge from the navy! I had a line in *Light Up the Sky* just before my character's entrance where he'd say, "Magic time!" It certainly was.

I learned a big lesson from my walk in the Black Forest that Christmas Day. When the doors open, we must walk through them.

SIX
CASA MAÑANA: MI INICIO

My time in the army was getting short. I finished up doing plays and such in Munich and was able to do a lot of sightseeing in Bavaria and Austria. I think Vienna is my favorite place. It is so beautiful, and the Viennese are very welcoming. There is a section there where Beethoven, Bach, Brahms, and Mozart all lived. It reminded me of Greenwich Village. It was near there where I went skiing for the first time at a resort located near Hitler's vacation home where he and Eva Braun cavorted. I experienced many wonderful things in Europe like the Maria Theresa Kunst der Haus, the castles of Prince Ludwig, the canals of Venice, and tracking Sputnik racing across the night sky over St. Mark's Square. Europe was everything I wanted it to be, but it was time to go home. We sailed from Liverpool on the *General Geiger*.

After several days of rough seas, we cheered as we entered New York Harbor and got our first glimpse of Miss Liberty and the New York skyline. It put lumps in our throats. I went directly to LaGuardia Airport and took the first plane to Love Field in Dallas, Texas. Some guys kissed the tarmac after we disembarked. I don't remember doing that, but I was glad to be home. Well, it wasn't so much home anymore. Mom, Dad, and my eighteen-year old brother, Dan, had left Dallas and moved to Van Buren, Arkansas.

I hooked up with my college roommate, Bob Porter, and his wife, Pat. They were the ones that had sent me the autographed photo of Lynda Bird Johnson, which helped me many times in passing inspections. At that time, Bob was a writer for the entertainment section in the *Dallas Times Herald*. I asked him if there was anyone hiring bright, talented actors who had no professional experience but were anxious to learn. He told me there was a man named Michael Pollack who was the managing director at Casa Mañana, a theater Fort Worth. I filed that information in my mind under "Slim to None," since Casa was mainly a musical venue. I couldn't carry a tune since my soprano voice

had changed at age thirteen. I decided to visit my alma mater in Denton.

I saw several of my professors, who were sympathetic, but had no ideas. As I was leaving, I had a wild hair. I decided to go over to the auditorium, hoping that the head of the opera department, Mary McCormic, would be there.

The McCormic family had made millions on heavy equipment such as the McCormic Reaper, and while Mary had kept the McCormic name, she was actually married to an Italian prince. She was also an internationally famous operatic soprano, tough as nails, and, I hoped, full of helpful advice.

I slipped quietly into the back of the auditorium, and sure enough, a cloud of smoke was rising from a long Bette Davis-esque cigarette holder. Left center, aisle seat, was Mary's perch. A break was soon called, and I decided to make my move.

Mary was dismissing someone as I approached her. When she saw me, her face lit up. We were fond of one another and occasionally had a cocktail together, but she had a fiery temper and you never knew when she would explode. I was lucky, thank God.

"What are you doing here?" she asked. "Who's defending the country?"

We exchanged hugs.

"I came to see you, of course," I said. "You're still my girl, aren't you?"

She looked at me suspiciously, lit up another Marlboro and motioned me to sit next to her. She wasted no time.

"What are you going to do about your acting?"

"Bob Porter told me that they are doing some plays at Casa Mañana this spring. Some guy named Michael Pollack is directing. I thought I'd give him a ring, set up an appointment."

"No!"

I was startled.

"Why not?" I asked.

"I'll tell you why. It's too damn easy to say no on the phone! Put on your best coat and tie and go over there tomorrow and don't leave until you meet that Pollack guy. Now get your butt out of here . . . and iron your shirt."

So I did.

The next morning, I put on my only coat and tie and appeared at Mr. Pollack's office. The door was open, and I could hear a typewriter clacking away. I gave my tie one more tug and entered. There was an attractive young woman typing. I walked over to her desk and waited until she looked up, smiled, and spoke.

"May I help you?" she asked.

I smiled back eagerly.

"Yes, I'd like to see Mr. Pollack, please."

"Do you have an appointment?"

"I'm sorry, I don't. I just flew in from Europe and New York."

"My, you've been a busy boy. Any of that true?"

I could feel my face turning crimson.

"It's almost all true. Sort of. I just got out of the army."

She thought for a moment.

I felt foolish. I was about to thank her and go.

"Mr. Pollack doesn't have an appointment this morning. He may not come in at all, unless . . ."

"Unless?" I blurted out.

"Sometimes he comes in to collect his mail. If you want to wait . . . I can't promise anything."

"No, that's fine, I'll wait. My schedule happens to be wide open today."

We both laughed.

I sat on a little bench. It seemed like a long time, but Michael Pollack walked in and picked up his mail at precisely 9:00 a.m. It must have been force of habit. He smiled and nodded in my direction.

As he rifled through his mail, he turned to his secretary and asked, "Anybody scheduled for me to meet today?"

She looked straight at me and said, "Just that gentleman sitting over there, Mr. Pollack."

With that, Michael Pollack walked over, shook my hand vigorously, and ushered me into his office. I shot a look to the secretary that said *thank you sooooooooo much.*

Michael and I hit it off immediately. He encouraged me to talk about college and life in the army, and we ended up discussing the really strange jobs we had both held in the past. He shared with me his days as a struggling musician in New York. One story in particular was hilarious. Pollack's agent had called to tell him he had been hired by the Central Park Zoo to play a French horn to the American alligators because it was mating season, and apparently, French horn music aroused their libidos.

After that, my story about shilling for the dart-throwing game seemed weak, but he thought it was a riot.

Mike told me that Casa had a couple of comedies and a few musicals on their schedule, including one which would be a world premiere. Then he asked if I thought I could play a corporal in the US Army. I told him it would be quite a stretch since private first class was as high as I ever reached in the military. Mike laughed again and then told me I had the part of Corporal Bohun in *Operation Mad Ball.* My head started spinning a little.

Then, out of nowhere, he asked if I could dance.

I decided to stall by asking, "Dance? Do you mean ballroom, classical, boogie-woogie, ballet, soft shoe . . . ?"

A blank stare.

"No. You know . . . choreographed numbers."

"Well, I did some square dancing in high school, but that's about it."

"Perfect! Can you sing?"

"About as well as I can dance," I said.

With that, Pollack walked over to the grand piano and began to play.

"Do you know this one?"

"Nope."

"How about this one?"

"Can't say that I do."

"Jim, that was the national anthem."

We went on like this for a few minutes. He would plunk out a tune, ask if it sounded familiar to me and I would shake my head no.

Exhausted, he said, "What about 'Old Man River'?" Everyone knows that one. You should be about here."

Mike gave me an arpeggio. At least, that's what I thought it was. I cleared my throat and began.

Old man river,
That old man river,
He must know sumpin',
But don't say nuthin',
He just keeps rollin',
He keeps on rollin' along.
He don't plant taters,
He don't plant cotton,
And them that plants 'em
Is soon forgotten,
But old man river . . .
(Mike joined in the big finish)

27

In the Casa Mañana production of *Calamity Jane*. *Courtesy of Casa Mañana Inc.*

More fun at Casa Mañana. *Courtesy of Casa Mañana Inc.*

He just keeps rollin'
He keeps on rollin' . . . along!

Mike had tears in his eyes. He was, after all, a musician. I was hired for four shows. Go figure. Thus began my career at Casa Mañana.

Our lighting designer that spring and summer of 1961, Jules Fisher, was a genius graduate of Carnegie Tech and I am proud to have called him a lifelong friend. It was his task to light the plays and musicals from just about every direction. Casa Mañana was a geodesic dome erected in 1936 as part of a Texas centennial celebration. The stage at Casa was round, with no back wall. Blocking for the actors included a good deal of movement and speaking loudly.

Sal Mineo, our lead in *Operation Mad Ball*, had had a career in movies in Hollywood where sound technicians made sure the audience heard the dialogue. A very small microphone is often clipped to a lapel or under a tie. From that point, the wire is attached to a small battery pack and sent to a soundboard. So Sal was one of the first stars that was miked for the stage. It worked like a charm. Most of the time.

While I was onstage in a scene with another actor, Sal was offstage for a few minutes. In the middle of our scene, something strange began to come through the loudspeakers in the theater. At first, it was a muffled humming noise. Then, we heard the undeniable metallic zip of a zipper. Here's how the next few moments played out:

1. The sound of a forceful stream of water.
2. Whistling over the continued sound of the stream.
3. Several loud bangs on a door.
4. The click of a door latch.
5. Frantic whispering then . . .
6. Sal Mineo's voice, "Holy cripes!"
7. Audience ovation.

We were sold out every night.

I hope there are still summer stock audiences in America that can forgive young people who are honing their craft. I did the best I could and loved every minute of it. I performed in four productions at Casa Mañana

With Casa Mañana darling Ruta Lee. *Author Collection.*

and got my actor's Equity card that summer. I was even one of the leads in the world premiere of *Calamity Jane*. Like *Operation Mad Ball*, it had been a movie first and then a stage production. My part was the role of Francis Friar, a variety artiste who could neither sing nor dance.

Sound familiar?

Thanks Michael Pollack. I'd like to think you are somewhere out there still serenading alligators with your French horn.

SEVEN
NEW YORK: TAKE TWO

First publicity photos, New York City.
Author Collection.

lit out for New York again, only this time I was armed with my brand-new Equity card. I was a real actor who got real money to act. Broadway here I come! Two weeks later I was standing in line at the unemployment bureau.

I was down to my last thirty dollars, which would not last much longer than three or four weeks. While standing in line, I noticed a young man who was passing out tickets for a new game show. I took one and in a few minutes several of the jobless, including myself, were being ushered into a theater. We were welcomed by a warm-up guy who encouraged us to be highly animated. For those of us who showed interest in being a contestant on the show, there was a form to fill out. *What the heck*, I thought. *What have I got to lose?* It was a fun show, and I enjoyed it. Afterwards, I was asked to stay a few minutes. I was told I had been chosen to be a contestant the following day. The show, then and now, is called *Password*. This was just what I needed to lift my spirits.

I was up against a nice lady from Queens (or someplace like that). I remember Allen Ludden making us welcome. The two celebrities that day were Chuck Connors and some Broadway star like Arlene Francis. I ended up winning three hundred dollars and a set of encyclopedias, which I promptly sold to a bookstore down the street for $150. Years later, I appeared on *Password* again, but as one of the celebrities. As far as I know, I'm the only actor who can brag about that one.

There is an old saying that goes, "Sit on a curb in New York City and sooner or later everyone you know will pass by." After running into Neal Weaver on Avenue C and Ninth Street, I became a believer. Neal was a fellow I'd met while in the army in Germany. We got along fine, but Neal was the sort of person who, when we learned we were going to Bavaria, taught himself German. I'm the sort of person who thinks of a great idea, but I never get around to actually following through. You wouldn't believe how long I worked on this book!

Neal the actor/writer/director/Northwestern alum did me two great services. Besides allowing me to crash on his couch until I found my own digs, he talked me out of buying a Lambretta motor scooter. Instead, he suggested that I could use the money from *Password* and join Michael Howard's acting class. Fortunately for me, I took his advice.

I auditioned for and was accepted into Michael's class. He was a wonderful teacher and encouraged his actors to take chances. One evening he passed along a story to the class that I've never forgotten. He told us that he had seen a sign outside a church and that if we never remembered anything else he taught us, to remember what the sign had said: "A ship is safest in port, but that is not what a ship is for."

On break at The Orchidia. *Author Collection.*

Michael held his classes above a small theater. Being there opened my eyes to some enormously talented actors in a play called *The Blacks*. Virtually every person in the cast went on to have their own television show or became big-time movie stars like James Earl Jones, Godfrey Cambridge, Esther Rolle, Cicely Tyson, and Louis Gossett Jr., to name a few. I got a bartender job in an Italian restaurant called The Orchidia just a block away, which was run by a Ukrainian lady named Mushka. It was a hangout for actors, including Eli Wallach and Anne Jackson, who were starring in two one-act plays called *The Typist* and *The Tiger*. Eli and Anne came in every night and ordered a medium pizza with mushrooms and extra cheese. Eli lived to be ninety-eight. Might be a good idea to add mushrooms to your diet.

I was becoming a New Yorker. My apartment was within a block of my job, my best friend Jules, my acting class, the subway, and the best chocolate egg cream in the world. Occasionally, I would get a job from Jules hanging lights or painting scenery for Bill McCauley, another pal from my college days. Sometimes, I would get a job posing as the husband who was unaware of his wife's infidelity for the romance magazines. I was content. All of this was about to change.

We had just finished our acting class when a lovely young woman thrust a folded note into my hand. Her name was Molly. She had that fresh-scrubbed folk-singer look, and indeed she was. I opened the folded piece of paper.

"Call this guy. He's making a short-subject film and you are perfect for the male lead."

I thanked Molly and called the guy the next morning. His name was Hayward Anderson. He told me to meet him at his office downtown.

I read for him right away. It was a boy-*wants*-to-meet-girl story set in Manhattan. Hayward was very frank. He told me it was between me and another guy, a phrase I had certainly heard before and would hear many times in the years to come. I could tell he was leaning towards the other guy, the bane of all actors. I knew that I had to keep him talking because if he had an opportunity to put his arm on my shoulder, walk me to the door, and thank me for coming, I would be a goner.

Me: "So, is this your first film?"

Hayward: "Yeah, it's something I always . . . "

Me: "I know what you mean. Who's doing the sets?"

Hayward: "You're looking at him. Why?"

Me: "It's something I do when things are slow."

Hayward: "Are things slow right now?"

Me: "That depends. There is some interest in my starring in a short movie."

Hayward: (laughter) "You don't waste any time, do you? How much for being the male star in my little movie?"

Me: "Here's an idea. How about I do both? Acting and set building for, say, $1,500?"

Academy Award Night Crab Artichoke Dip

The envelope please. And the award goes to . . .

INGREDIENTS

1 can quartered artichoke hearts (not marinated)

1 cup Hellman's mayonnaise (Do NOT substitute with salad dressing)

1 cup Kraft parmesan cheese (Do NOT use freshly grated)

1 cup lump crab meat (be sure to remove all shell bits)

DIRECTIONS

Preheat oven to 350 degrees. Drain artichoke hearts, discard liquid, and chop lightly. Mix all ingredients and place them in a shallow baking dish. Bake until bubbly. Serve with toasted baguette or Cabernet crackers.

Note: You can double this recipe, and leave out the crab, if so desired.

New York "take two" publicity shot. *Author Collection.*

Hayward: "Deal. Let's shake on it. We'll build our apartment set in a vacant garage in Mount Vernon. The outside shots and the subway we'll just shoot until the cops run us off. Fortunately, I know most of them, so I'm not too concerned about that. Our budget is five grand."

Me: "Where did you get the dough?"

Hayward: "I'm a bartender in Greenwich Village."

Me: "What are you going to call this epic?"

Hayward: "*One Plus One.*"

We shot the film in three days. It was a hoot, but in a few weeks I forgot all about it.

I knew how to wear a lot of hats, so I booked a play working as both assistant stage manager and prop man, along with the role of an FBI agent in the third act. We opened at the Paper Mill Playhouse in New Jersey with a wonderful cast: Tom Poston, Elizabeth Allen, Louise Lasser (who was dating Woody Allen at the time), Renée Taylor, and Bill Hickey. The play was hilarious, and we all believed we were a cinch for Broadway. We closed after two weeks in Yonkers.

I went back to my job as waiter/bartender for Mushka at The Orchidia. It did, after all, serve the best Italian food on the Lower East Side, and Mushka made sure I ate for free. It was a great place for hungry actors. Notables like Allen Ginsberg, who wrote *Howl*, were regulars. Mushka was like my mom. She told me I would always have a job there when I needed one, and she was there when I received some astounding news. The little short-subject film which I had completed months earlier had changed its title to *The Cliff Dwellers* and had been nominated for an Oscar. I received my tickets to the Academy Awards and had just two weeks to prepare for the night that every actor dreams of.

EIGHT
HOORAY FOR HOLLYWOOD!

Suddenly, I had to start thinking of the millions of things I needed to do to get ready for the trip to Los Angeles, not the least of which was airfare from New York to LAX. Thank God for Flying Tigers Airlines (round-trip fare was only $180). My friend Bill McCauley threw me a party and got me to the airport in plenty of time. I waved goodbye, checked my bags, and awaited the boarding call. Our flight departure time came and went. "Just a small problem," we were told. Twice we were loaded and unloaded. Finally, they told us we would leave the following day.

I had to find a pay phone to call Bill to come get me as Flying Tigers was closing for the night. It was a quiet trip back to Manhattan from LaGuardia. Hangovers were asserting themselves. There is no good way to say goodbye twice in a twenty-four-hour period. I lay low most of the rest of that day. Bill insisted on taking me to the airport again, but the goodbyes were more subdued this time. The flight was only three hours late, but it was full, and the props were spinning merrily. Several hours later, we landed in Chicago. I didn't remember Chicago being on the itinerary but guessed that they needed gas. We deplaned and were told to stay near the gate for what would be "only a few minutes." Some of our merry troop were becoming dubious, myself included.

In short order, I found a bar in the terminal where I struck up a conversation with a fellow actor who was on my flight. I thought I recognized him. He had made a few commercials in New York and thought it was time to venture out West.

We talked about agents—I, about The Kohner Agency and he, about William Morris. Between the time I got the notice that *The Cliff Dwellers* had been nominated and the trip out to Los Angeles for the awards, I had received a letter from an agent who said he would like to represent me on the West Coast. At first I thought some of my pals were playing a joke. So, I called my buddy Pat Boone. He had already completed his second or third movie by then.

I asked him if he had heard of an agent by the name of Paul Kohner.

"I wish he was my agent," he said.

That sounded like good news. So, I had made an appointment to see Mr. Kohner while I was in Los Angeles.

My actor friend was in the middle of an interesting story about having to smoke two entire cartons of Chesterfields during a commercial shoot when I happened to look out the window and notice that our plane was taxiing down the runway. We dropped some cash on the counter and bolted toward the gate. We ran yelling and waving, attempting to get their attention. A cyclone fence stopped us from running out on the tarmac, but we continued to jump up and down, gesturing for them to wait. Our plane was lifting off the runway. It was going to Los Angeles without us. We watched in silence. It was devastating. We looked at each other, somehow feeling as though it was our fault, and then . . . was the plane banking to the left? It was! They had discovered they were short two passengers! *I bet it was that cute stewardess I flirted with that noticed our absence,* I thought.

Sure enough, it made two giant U-turns and touched down. We waved and laughed and then waved some more. We were laughing and doing a little hoedown when we noticed it was gaining speed again. We were stumped. We started yelling again. The plane was climbing and beginning to make a gigantic right turn. There was only one thing to do. I was solemn and controlled.

"We must alert the tower," I said. "Obviously our pilot is drunk."

We climbed the tower stairs and opened the unlocked door. One of the three puzzled men spoke.

Tower Guy: "Who the hell are you?"

Me: "I'm a passenger, Sir. There is a pilot in that Flying Tiger that must be intoxicated."

Tower Guy: "How did you come to that conclusion, Bright Eyes? Did you smell his breath from way up here? Seems to me you boys are the ones who have been imbibing."

Me: "He has taken off and landed two or three times in the last half hour! Don't you care about our safety?"

Tower Guy: "Your safety is paramount at Flying Tiger. The flight is not leaving without you. Your copilot is just taking a test that will license him should it be necessary for him to take the captain's chair. Have a good flight. They'll be reloading passengers shortly. Oh, the weather might be a little bumpy."

Imagine that! All that running around jumping and yelling over a pilot that needed a license to fly! We had a good laugh. I was looking forward to a little shut-eye. I asked for a blanket and went to sleep almost immediately. Soon I was awakened by the cute stewardess (as opposed to the cranky stewardess). She was making sure we had our seatbelts buckled as the plane was tossing about a bit. I looked out my porthole. We were in some rough weather. We were going in and out of clouds and I could see that we were in a huge storm. I'd never had any motion sickness in my life, but I was a getting a little queasy. Almost everyone was using their little barf bags. Only three of us were keeping our dinners down. Even the cute stew was suddenly not so adorable. She was unable to render help.

My new actor pal, the cranky stew, and I were able to make sure everyone had air-sick bags. The bad news was that as they ran out of bags, there was nothing to do but reuse them. When we finally landed, the cute stew quit her job right on the spot. Unfortunately, she vomited a quart or two on me before I could get out of the way.

I was picked up by Don Henley, an old friend of Pat Boone's. I cleaned myself as best I could, but I was fragrant even with the windows rolled down. We made it to Don's apartment just off the Sunset Strip. He handed me the keys, and I enjoyed the best hour-long shower of my life. Don stayed at a friend's until the fumes weakened. Fortunately, Pat had a beautiful and sweet-smelling tuxedo.

Don's place happened to be only two blocks away from The Kohner Agency, and since I was newly clean, I thought I might pop in on my new agent. I almost bumped into another client, Anjelica Huston, as I entered. Walter Kohner took me into the office of Paul Kohner, who rose and shook my hand. He smiled broadly and turned to Walter.

"What a punim. Isn't there something for this guy?"

Walter turned to me and said, "He likes your face, your punim."

Can I ride a horse? Of course! *Author Collection.*

"I know," I answered. "I'm the Shabbos goy in my building."

Walter asked me if I could ride a horse. I pointed out that I was from Texas. He looked at his watch.

"Let's beat the traffic," he said.

He drove seventy miles per hour while weaving expertly in and out of the lanes on the 101. We pulled up to a building in Studio City which housed the offices of Stalmaster-Lister, casting agents to *Gunsmoke.* I was handed a script with a one-word title, "Jeb."

Jim Lister shook my hand and said, "Read the part of Jeb."

I had read only a few pages when I was called into Norman Macdonnell's office. Harry Harris, the director, looked a little unhappy.

Harry: "Can you ride a horse?"

Me: "I'm from Texas, Sir."

Harry: "Walter tells me your short-subject film is nominated. Did you ride a horse?"

Me: "No, Sir. It takes place in New York City. I rode the subway."

Jim Lister and Norman laughed, but Harry was unmoved.

After what appeared to be a disastrous audition and first impression with my new agency, Walter drove us back to Beverly Hills . . . in silence. We pulled into the parking lot and entered the office.

Walter: "How did it go?"

Me: "Okay, I guess Mr. Kohner. Thanks a lot."

Walter: "When are you going back to New York?"

Me: "Monday. I don't want to lose my job."

Walter: "I see. Well, you might think it over. Monday's no good, see, because you'll be working. You got the part. Just pays scale though, $750. That all right?"

I nodded in the affirmative.

Walter: "It's the number one show in the country."

I nodded.

Mr. Kohner had a phone in his hand.

Walter: "Okay, you bank robbers, but this is the last time Mr. Hampton works for scale. He's got a big job in New York!"

Now that's an agent!

The day after I moved to Los Angeles to seek my fame and fortune, I did what any red-blooded American did. I applied for unemployment. While I was standing in line, I couldn't help eavesdropping on a conversation between two actors in front of me. It went something like this:

Actor Number 1: "Is this not the worst season ever?"

Actor Number 2: "Brutal. I can't remember things being this slow. No work. Nada. Nothing."

My heart sank. These two guys seemed to be professionals. How was I going to make it? I was thinking I ought to get out of line and hitch a ride back to New York. Then, I heard one more comment:

Actor Number 1: "I'll tell you how bad it is. I'm not going to be able to pay my pool guy!"

I stopped in my tracks. I thought if cleaning your own swimming pool is as bad as it gets in Hollywood, maybe I'll just stick around.

The night of the Academy Awards was magic. Pat lent me his Caddie convertible for the evening. The show took place in an auditorium in Santa Monica. I had picked up Molly from a friend's place in West Hollywood, as I recall. A red carpet had been unrolled with Army Archerd at the head. He wished us good luck. Our seats were on the aisle, lest we won and needed to hurry down to the stage. The entertainment was terrific. Everything from an eighteen-year-old Ann-Margret to the pipes of Ethel Merman singing, you guessed it, "There's No Business Like Show Business!" They were wearing radio mikes (a brand-new innovation), although I'm not sure Ethel needed hers. Gregory Peck (who was like a god to me), won the Best Actor Oscar for *To Kill a Mockingbird*.

"Will Act For Food." *Author Collection.*

Molly and I weren't winners that night, but we took away many warm, wonderful memories. After the presentations for the awards and the end of the entertainment, we learned we were invited to the after party at the Beverly Hilton. There was a complete orchestra, and Molly thought one last dance was in order. The next thing I knew, we were swirling around the floor. It was a perfect ending to a fairy tale. Molly was leaving in the morning to meet her intended back in New York, and I was to begin work the following Monday on *Gunsmoke*. At that moment, I bumped into someone. When I turned around, it was Gregory Peck. I began to beg forgiveness for my clumsiness.

"Nonsense. It was my fault," he said. "By the way, I saw your film. You were very good, young man."

"I saw your film too, Sir," I replied. "You're not so bad yourself."

He roared with laughter and danced away. I had made Gregory Peck laugh!

The following Monday I began shooting on *Gunsmoke*. I was amazed that the hour-long Westerns were filmed in only five days. I was curious as to how the director, Harry Harris, would be able to pull it off. I soon learned. We came early and stayed late, and we had the best cast and crew on television. I was nervous, and to be honest, so was Harry.

The filming would take place in Gower Gulch. It was, and still is, named that because so many Westerns were shot on lots on or near Gower Street in Hollywood. My call time for makeup and wardrobe was for 6:30 a.m. I was a half hour early because I was so nervous that I couldn't sleep anyway. I got a steaming cup of black coffee and took time to walk around the soundstages. They were huge. For example, both the interior and the exterior of Miss Kitty's Long Branch Saloon were contained inside just one of the soundstages. This would allow the gaffer to change the lighting in minutes from daylight to dark, depending on the script. In Hollywood, time is definitely money.

I had a little trailer with my name on the door. Inside there was a couch, a lighted mirror, a stool and a toilet. As I was taking all this in, I thought, *Jimmy, this is what you have worked and dreamed for. At this moment, you've arrived. Don't do anything to screw it up.*

There was a knock on my door. I opened it to a huge man who introduced himself as Tiny, the third assistant director. He was delivering "sides." I had a script but learned that sides were the pages that would be shot first. Tiny asked if I had eaten breakfast.

I shook my head. He recommended the breakfast burrito.

I figured a guy who was three hundred pounds plus would know what was good to eat. So, I began my first day with a burrito in one hand and sides in the other.

An intern came to fetch me to get into wardrobe and visit hair and makeup. Patty Whiffing was in charge of hair, and I think Glen Randall took care of makeup. They were both delightful people, as was everyone who was involved in the number one show in the world. I was introduced to the cast, and then we were assembled on the set. Harry and the crew were already positioning the camera and deciding which lenses to use.

It was a "master" shot, which was my entrance through the swinging doors up to the bar where Glenn Strange (who once played Frankenstein's monster) served me a stein of beer that I downed immediately because I was thirsty. Got it so far? After I drained the mug, I headed to the free lunch and I collided with the bad guy, Buck Young. He takes a swing but misses me. Simple, right?

This is called camera blocking. Just before we tried one, I asked Glenn what was in my beer glass.

"Beer," he replied. "It's cheap and foamy. We've tried other stuff, but the only thing that looks like beer is beer."

Before we got it all right and Harry was satisfied, I had chugged eleven beers and had knocked over two chairs and a table. Roy Thinnes, the good guy, saved me from the bad guy, and we got applause from the cast and crew when Harry said, "Cut, print!"

Tiny helped me to my trailer and I fell asleep on my couch. I called my mom that evening.

Mom: "How did it go?"
Me: "Well, I got drunk and got into a fight!"
Mom: "You better be lying to me."
Me: "Do you know what a 'burrito' is?"
Mom: "Sounds like a jackass."
Me: "They eat 'em for breakfast."
Mom: "Well, if that don't beat the hens a-peckin'!"
Me: "Love you, Mom. I'll call tomorrow."

That's the way the rest of the week went. What a wonderful group, these people assembled as the cast of *Gunsmoke.* Amanda Blake, our housemother (not unlike Miss Kitty) loved a good joke. Then there was Milburn Stone (Doc) who could always make the dialogue more realistic. Millie was a doctor who healed scripts. Dennis Weaver (Deputy Chester Goode) was destined to have his own show. Jim Arness was the star who wouldn't act like one. Arness could pretend without pretense. And the wonderful Ken Curtis as Festus. To my surprise, I was invited back for another Jeb role and as another character Eliab, who was Festus's nephew. In that role, all my character wanted to do was shoot off Ken's ear . . . or at least "the little hangy-down part."

Years later I asked Harry Harris what the circumstances were around my being hired in the first place. Harry was completely candid. He didn't want to hire me. I had virtually no camera experience, and as far as television was concerned, I had no experience at all. He'd had another actor in mind. God bless Jim Lister, the casting agent who adamantly declared he would resign from casting if I wasn't hired for the role of Jeb. I had never known that Jim stood up for me, and I was never able to thank him properly. I hope he is in casting heaven. I will always be in Harry's debt as well. The stories I am privileged to relate to you will, I hope, show why we actors are addicted to entertaining folks. It is my hope that you will be entertained as well.

NINE
ALWAYS GOOD FOR A LAUGH

An excited young actor makes the following entry in his diary:

> Dear Diary,
>
> At last! A chance to show my talent. All of the dreary jobs I've performed for this company over the summer have been worth it. All I have been hoping and praying for is an opportunity to do my thing. Well, here is my chance. Marvin Del Rio, the star of the Sommerset Players here in Nantucket has laryngitis! Tonight I will go on as his understudy! There is a scene at the close of the second act that is so powerful! I am downstage, center stage, delivering a dramatic monologue. There isn't even anyone else on the stage except the old character actor who has no lines. In fact, he is all the way upstage with his back to the audience, sitting at a desk writing. Tomorrow I will be a star!

The next entry reads:

> Dear Diary,
> He drank the ink!

Two actors run into each other at a New York restaurant.

"Joe! Where you been? I haven't seen you around."

"I've been touring with *The Producers*."

"Oh yeah? How'd it go?"

"Great! Incredible! We started in Philly, held over for six weeks. Boffo business! Then we did three months in San Francisco. Unbelievable reviews! Standing room only every night. Chicago was next. They held a parade! We got keys to the city! We cried when we left there. Then we played Detroit. They just didn't get it there. Lukewarm reviews. We papered the houses. Nothing worked. We closed after three weeks."

"Oh yeah, I heard about Detroit."

John Wayne decided to try his hand at Shakespeare. He had always wanted to be appreciated for his acting talent, and when he learned Hamlet didn't have to ride a horse, he was sold. He worked for weeks memorizing his lines and trying to develop a British theatrical accent. Alas, it didn't work out very well. The opening night's audience was peppered with his friends and acquaintances. They were polite for a while, but by the time he got to Hamlet's famous soliloquy, they had begun to show their displeasure with a few boos and hisses. The Duke soldiered on.

"Tuh be, er . . . not tuh be," (boos.) "Wull, that's the question," (boos and hisses) "Whether it's nobler in the . . . eyes a men…"

People began shouting, "You're a disgrace! Get off the stage!"

John had the last word.

"Well, hey. Don't blame me. I didn't write this crap!"

An actor returned to his home after spending the day walking the picket lines in support of striking writers. As he approached his house in Tarzana, he saw fire trucks, police cars, and an ambulance in his driveway. The firemen were wrapping up what appeared to be a fire at his house. He jumped out of his car just as the paramedics were loading his wife into an ambulance. He rushed to his wife's side and asked what had happened.

"It was awful!" She sobbed. "Your agent came to the house. He was drunk and crazy. He shot the dog, tried to strangle me, and set the house on fire!"

The actor took in this information for a moment then replied, "I can't believe it! My agent . . . came to the house!"

This following story is dedicated to the traveling tent shows that brought theater to cities and towns all over Texas in the thirties and forties. In particular, it is dedicated to the Madcap Players who performed in Dallas at Fair Park in 1939.

I was only three years old, but I remember everything about that night. The streetcar ride to Fair Park, the tent, the stage, the colorful lights, and the glorious smell of the sawdust on the grounds, just like the circus. The play was a drawing-room comedy with women in fashionable gowns accepting cigarettes in silver cases from men in tuxedos. The leading man looked like a sissy with his lipstick and rouge on his face, not to mention a penciled-on mustache. The opening act was a cocktail party held by the leading lady. The audience laughed at everything the leading man said, but I didn't think he was so hot. My attention was on the leading lady.

Next to my mother, I thought she was the most beautiful creature on earth. It was her I dreamed of as I fell asleep in Mama's lap before the first-act curtain.

A tent show like the one I described above was doing the circuit through south central Texas performing their play *The Jealous Husband*. It was a three-act potboiler about an older rich man who obsessed over his young wife. The trucks were being unloaded when Trish, the ingénue of the company, approached the stage manager, Will, with bad news. She was running a fever and had seen a doctor who had forbidden her from performing that evening.

"I know I've put you in a bad spot Will, but the sawbones told me I have walking pneumonia. I'm supposed to stay in bed till the fever breaks. How are you going to find a replacement this late?" she asked.

"You leave that to me. I'll think of something."

"But I'm feeling a little better now. I just took my temperature. It's going down a little bit."

Will knew she was lying.

"What's your temperature now?"

She hung her head.

"One hundred five . . . but . . . "

"But nothing! You get to bed. I'll check on you later.

We are going on if I have to put on a dress and do the part myself!"

He had tried to cheer her up, but he was whistling past the graveyard. Will walked over to the square. He sat down on a bench in front of the drugstore and lit up a Lucky. He wished there was a saloon in town, but like many other counties in the Southwest, it was dry. Lost in his thoughts, he didn't see her approach until she spoke.

"Got a light cowboy?"

Will glanced up to see an attractive blonde woman with a big smile and an unlit Chesterfield. He got an idea: Trish is only in three scenes. We've got two hours till curtain. We could get in at least one rehearsal. If she had to, she could read her lines from the script. It just might work!

"Lady, how would you like to make twenty bucks?"

Wanda Sue was a natural. She was very confident and even changed some of her lines slightly to suit her, and they worked even better. The tent was full that night. At her first entrance in Act One, Wanda Sue got a rousing hand and a few whistles. Will attributed it to "local girl makes good," but Randolph, the leading man, was so flummoxed he "went up.'" His line was "Just where have you been, Loretta?"

When he didn't say it, Wanda Sue turned to him and ad-libbed, "Don't you want to know where I've been?"

Randy nodded dumbly and Wanda Sue added, "Well it's none of your beeswax!"

It stopped the show.

Toward the end of the third act, there is a terrible argument between Wanda Sue's character and her drunken sot of a husband (played by Randy), who mistakenly believes she is having an affair with her chauffeur and shoots her in a jealous frenzy. The audience gasped audibly and many were moved to tears.

As the curtain slowly descended, Randy uttered his final torturous line, as he slumped to his knees, "What have I done, oh what have I done?"

A man in the audience rose and with tears streaming down his face shouted, "I'll tell you what you have done, you drunk bastard! You just killed the only whore in Waxahachie!"

Punchline Punch

INGREDIENTS

½ cup sugar

1 cup water

½ teaspoon whole cloves

3 2-inch cinnamon sticks

2 cups cranberry juice cocktail

½ cup lemon juice

1 cup orange juice (pulp-free)

1 quart ginger ale

Fresh orange and lemon slices

Additional whole cloves

DIRECTIONS

Mix the first four ingredients in a saucepan. Bring to a boil and let boil for 5 minutes. Strain out the spices and set aside to cool. Mix the spices and sugar water with fruit juices. Pour into a punch bowl over ice just before serving. Add ginger ale. Stud lemon and orange slices with remaining whole cloves and float in punch.

Pour into punch cup.

Stick out pinky finger.

Slurp.

Serves 12.

TEN

AGENTS, YOUR PERSONAL PITCHMEN

Groucho Marx is credited with the line, "I don't want to belong to any golf club that would accept me as a member." It's the same with theatrical agents. The one that wants you is never as desirable as the one who won't sign you. I have been very lucky with agents, but there were a few stinkers along the way. It is with great pleasure that I can relate this story about one of the stinkiest.

All actors have wide swings in their careers. There are times when you get everything that comes your way, and there are times when you cannot get arrested, as the saying goes. It was one of those lean times for me. I had switched to a larger, flashier agency in the hopes that it would jump-start my sputtering career, but so far it hadn't. When I first met with the agency, they assured me, due to their vast network of connections, that I'd never be idle. We had all congratulated ourselves over lunch in a trendy West Hollywood restaurant the day I signed. Weeks went by, however, with no evidence that anything was coming my way. When I called to chat with one of the agents, he would be on another call or away from his desk. I left messages, but my calls were never returned. I was thinking of a career in phone sales. Fortunately for me, in those days, actors who get a lead on something that another actor might benefit from shared the news.

I got a call from actor Ron Soble. Ron and I were golfing buddies and partners in many a game of bridge. He was also a fellow board member of the Screen Actors Guild, a tireless negotiator for better working conditions, and a pioneer in obtaining residuals for all actors. The phone call went like this:

Ron: "Jim? Ron. Do you ever read the trades?"

Me: "No."

Ron: "Why not?"

Me: "Because I don't know what they're talking about.

It's always somebody 'Jetting to Gotham to ink a pact,' or 'Sticks Nix Hicks Pix.'"

Ron: "Well, that's too bad, because sometimes there might be something of interest in them. Take today's *Hollywood Reporter,* for example."

Me: "There is something in today's *Reporter*? What is it?"

Ron: "Oh, something you might find very interesting. It might even concern you personally. It's on page three, as a matter of fact."

Me: "What? Read it to me."

Ron: (chuckling) "Oh no, I think it is important that you obtain a copy of today's *Hollywood Reporter* and read it for yourself."

Me: "I hate you." (click)

As I drove over to the news kiosk at Van Nuys and Ventura, I thought of all the ways I could make Ron's life miserable if this was some kind of sick joke. I pull up, get the paper, and open it to page three. The upper left-hand corner featured the following item of interest:

"Rex Sparger of Hitbound Productions is looking for a Jim Hampton/Paul Williams type for his pilot, *A Little Bit of Heaven.*"

I read it twice more. It went on to say that Mr. Sparger's office was in Venice Beach, California, and kindly provided his telephone number. I raced home (we didn't have cellular phones yet), hoping against hope that Paul Williams's agent was as useless as mine, and dialed the number.

Friendly receptionist: "Hitbound Productions."

Me: "May I speak to Mr. Sparger please?"

Friendly Receptionist: "Certainly, Sir. Who shall I say is calling?"

Me: "This is Jim Hampton calling."

The next person on the phone turns out to be Rex, a writer/producer from Oklahoma.

Rex: "Where are you, boy? We been lookin' all over for you!"

Me: "Well, I'm right here."

Rex: "We called AFTRA and they don't even know who your agent is!"

Me: "Just as well. He wouldn't return your calls."

Rex: "What?"

Me: "Just a little joke. Where do we go from here?"

Rex: "How long will it take you get down here?"

Me: "About half an hour depending on traffic."

That was that easy, but I had one more phone call to make. Here's how *that one* went.

Snooty Receptionist: "Fulla Baloney Agency, will you hold?"

Before I could answer she was gone. I held. A few minutes later:

Snooty Receptionist: "Thank you for holding. How may I direct your call?"

Me: "I would like to speak to Milo Krapp."

Snooty: "Thank you, and what is the nature of your call?"

Me: "My name is Hampton. I'm a client. I would like to speak to my agent."

Snooty: "I'm sorry, Mr. Hampton, it has just been a madhouse around here today. Mr. Krapp is in a meeting."

Me: "Sure. Tell him he's fired."

Snooty: "Well, I'm not sure I could . . . Oh, I see him coming out of the meeting now. Please hold while I ring."

Krapp: "Milo. Be brief."

Me: "This won't take a second, Milo. I just have a couple of questions."

Krapp: "Shoot."

Me: "Do you read the trades?"

Krapp: "Of course!"

Me: "Did you read them today?"

Krapp: "Yes. Look, I don't have . . ."

Me: "Just one more, Milo, I know you're a busy man. Did you happen to see anything in there for me?"

Krapp: "No. Nothing, nada, zip!"

Me: "You're fired. Now see, that didn't take long, did it?"

Denim overload on the pilot of *Force Five*, 1975. *Author Collection.*

Mr. Sparger had the contract ready to sign when I got there. It was one paragraph. The shortest contract I ever saw. All of the regulars were to receive $7,500 for the pilot, which would increase to $15,000 upon the sale of the pilot. Each of us would receive $15,000 per show for the first year. It was a good script and a fun show. I apologize for not remembering everyone in a cast that included Cleavon Little, Rue McClanahan, Peter Lawford, Ron Palillo, Jack Elam, and me. We were angels that ran a B&B in New England. When people needed help, we provided angelic assistance. Rex even hired my son, Jimmy, as an assistant prop man. The pilot didn't sell though. A few years later, however, there were shows on the air with a very similar format. Ever heard of *Newhart*?

Paul and Walter Kohner and Carl Forrest were the entire agent staff at The Kohner Agency. It was a pretty good agency, though. On any given day you might run into some of their clients like Lana Turner, John and Anjelica Huston, Greta Garbo, or Charles Bronson. The office was very conveniently situated in a little one-story building on Sunset Boulevard near Doheny. Some of the biggest agents in Hollywood today trained there and later went on to form their own very successful agencies. There was a bar across the street called The Cock and Bull that had sensational martinis. When I was in the neighborhood, I often stopped by the agency to find out if I still had a career. What I am about to tell you actually happened. I

"The King of Commercials."
Author Collection.

Only The Book and the Brick are Real

Send Money

have not changed one word.

One afternoon, finding myself in the vicinity, I popped into the agency. Carl Forrest, who handled much of the television side of things, was at his desk. Everyone else was at lunch.

"Hey Carl," I said, "Anything happening out there for me?"

"Vell," he said in his heavy Austrian accent, "as a matter of fact, I had a call about you today."

"Really? What'd they say?"

"Vell, a producer said he vas lookink for a Chim Hampton type."

"Well, what did you say?"

"I said, 'Congratulations! We handle Chim Hampton!'"

"Yeah, and . . . ?"

"He said, 'No. Ve don't vant Chim Hampton, just a Chim Hampton type.'"

ANIMAL ACTORS, AKA SCENE STEALERS

W. C. Fields once said something like, "Never work with children or animals." I know that Fields worked with an elephant in *The Great McConagall*, but as far as I know, he never worked with camels. I did. It was as a result of being cast in a movie called *Hawmps!* produced by Mulberry Square Productions out of my hometown of Dallas. They were the same folks who gave us *Benji*.

Benji was a big hit. *Hawmps!* was not.

Maybe it had something to do with the star of the picture. There certainly was plenty of talent in the supporting cast of Slim Pickens, Denver Pyle, Jack Elam, Chris Connelly, Herb Vigram, and others. The star . . . oh, what was his name? You know him. What was his name? Oh, yeah. Me. And did I mention camels?

Joe Camp, the director, took us all out to a ranch in Thousand Oaks, California, to meet up with our costars and allow us to get used to each other. I had heard a lot of bad things concerning camels. For one thing, they were constantly complaining with loud, indescribably nasty noises. The only sound I can compare it to might be the sounds you hear emitting from a fraternity latrine after a spring break kegger. I had also heard camels were dangerous and that they were able to kick in any direction. What I didn't know was they can also use their heads to give you a vicious whack. In fact, some months after filming, our head camel wrangler, Ray Chandler, suffered a broken neck from just such a blow. I had also heard that camels spit.

Unfortunately, none of these tales was even slightly exaggerated. There is a lot to watch out for when you are around these animals, but nothing can prepare you for the spitting. Camels chew their cud and have multiple stomachs, like cattle. When they are annoyed, and it doesn't take much to annoy one of these beasts, they can unleash a vile green stream that will put you off guacamole for life.

Benji, the famous pooch. *Author Collection.*

Buddy Denver Pyle and me in *Hawmps!*. *Courtesy of Joe Camp.*

In order to climb aboard a camel, you must get them into a "couched" position, which is all the way down in a sort of kneeling prone position. At that point you may easily mount. The camel that was chosen for me was Sheba. The movie was based on the introduction of camels into the United States Cavalry in the mid-nineteenth century, an actual historical event. Joe was a stickler for historical accuracy, and period McClellan cavalry saddles were used. They fit nicely on top of the dromedary's hump, and when you were astride, there was a view similar to that through the window of a second-story building. The first time I attempted to mount Sheba I put my left foot in the stirrup, but before I could swing my right leg over, the camel unexpectedly stood up. At that point, the view was exactly the same as that of being hung upside down from a second-story building. Nevertheless, it didn't take too long to establish a relationship with Sheba.

With Sheba in *Hawmps!*. Courtesy of Joe Camp.

Riding a camel is nothing like riding a horse. A horse needs to know who is boss. A camel already knows—it's the camel. Sheba would do what I asked of her when it suited her and when she was in the mood. The other camels were similar, but all seemed to have their own personalities. These attitudes caused many delays in filming. It was as if the camels belonged to their own union. When they were asked to do something, they sort of talked it over, voted, and took it from there.

After we had been filming for many weeks on location in Old Tucson, a group of professional Hollywood stuntmen appeared to film the arrival of the camels in the Old West. In the script, the camels caused a huge stir as no one had ever seen animals like them before. Horses were spooked, wagons were overturned, and general chaos ensued. Several cameras were positioned around the main street, and after much discussion and planning, everyone was ready to go . . . except the camels. They had gone on strike. Literally. They refused to budge from their couched positions. I believe the camels were thinking, *You know, we have spent several weeks training these yahoos, and what happens? They bring in a whole new crew for us to train. I don't think so.* They just sat there with the embarrassed stunt folk doing everything they knew to get them to budge. Finally, we all got

on our respective camels and did a rehearsal with them. They got the idea and were then quite willing to do it with the new guys.

We even had a baby camel. The trainer of *Benji*, Frank Inn, also had a way with camels. He had trained a baby camel to do the most amazing things. Her name was Valentine and she was definitely cute, cuddly, and smart. So, I wasn't working only with animals, I was working with a baby animal named Valentine. She could open doors, untie knots, and pick a bottle up and drink from it. The camera loved her. I appeared with Valentine on *The Mike Douglas Show, The Merv Griffin Show*, and even *The Tonight Show* with Johnny Carson. She was unimpressed with the celebrities and, without fail, relieved herself on camera to the delight of the audiences.

Nobody knew I was there.

W. C. Fields was a smart man.

The best show business animal story I ever heard was told to me by a director who swears it is gospel. The director, although not exactly a pal of mine, used me more than once in commercial shoots. We were swapping stories one day while we were waiting for the set to be lit. I had told him a couple of tales with an animal theme and he came up with this one:

Between scenes on *Hawmps!*. *Author Collection.*

I was contacted a few years ago about doing a commercial for a local bank. We had a lunch meeting where the idea for the commercial was pitched to me, and I must say it was an intriguing idea. What they wanted to emphasize was how easy it was to bank at their bank. It was so easy, according to the client, that a monkey could do it. They wanted to know if a chimpanzee could be trained to go through the motions of making a bank transaction. I said I didn't know, but it sounded like a helluva idea. I called up an animal trainer out in Thousand Oaks that I had worked with and told him the idea. He told me it could be done, but it would take several months because it involved six different behaviors: (1) The monkey must stand in line and wait his turn at the window. (2) He must approach the window. (3) He must give the teller his passbook. (4) He must take the pen that is offered by the teller and pretend to sign his name on a bank slip. (5) He must take back his passbook and the money the teller counts out to him. (6) He must turn left and walk out of the shot. I learned that he had a three-year-old chimp named Mickey who already knew how to roller

skate. That wasn't going to be necessary, but at least we knew he was a fast learner. The trainer believed he could accomplish the training in six months, but he needed to start immediately. I told the ad agency what I'd learned, and it was a go. Six months later we were on the bank set giving instructions to the humans who would be supporting players. The agency guys and the client were a little late, and I asked the trainer if I could see what the bank had been spending a lot of its good money on. I almost fell out of my chair when Mickey came on the set. He was named Mickey after Mickey Rooney, and I have to say there definitely was a resemblance. He was already in wardrobe—two-toned saddle oxfords, slacks, sport coat, bow tie, and a jaunty little pork pie hat. Cutest little guy you ever saw, but could he act?

We had an impromptu rehearsal. Before I called action for the rehearsal, the trainer leaned over and told me he'd thrown in something a little extra. I called action. Mickey waited in line, went to the window, gave the teller his passbook, scribbled his name, took his money, and tipped his hat. Pandemonium! Nobody had ever seen anything like it before.

About then, the client and the ad people show up. They apologize for being late, but there is no problem and we get ready for the take. The mood on the set is "we've really got a winner here." All the last-minute lighting adjustments are made with one of the little persons standing in for Mickey, and we are ready to roll. I was so proud that we were able to pull this off. I made a mental note to add a little something extra to the trainers check and . . . Action!

Mickey stands in line, gets to the window, hands the teller his passbook, signs his name, gets his dough, tips his hat, and exits camera left. Cut, print, perfect! I turn around beaming. As far as I'm concerned, we get reaction shots from the people in the bank and we're done, but the agency guy and the client are huddling.

The agency guy looks worried as he comes over. I ask him if there is a problem. He tells me Mickey is doing things too fast, that he's rushing. Mickey just needs to slow everything down. I'm searching the guy's face who is giving me tips on a chimp's performance. He's dead serious.

I walk over to the chimpanzee who is sitting in his own chair with "Mickey" written on the back and I kneel down. I tell him that everyone likes what he is doing. I tell him the thing with the hat is a riot, but he is going too fast. Maybe it's nerves. I told him to relax and have fun with it.

We go back to opening marks and get ready for take two. The agency guy tells the client about our little talk with Mickey. They are all smiling and nodding at each other and . . . Action!

Mickey waits in line, gets to the window, signs his slip, collects his dough, tips his hat, and exits stage left. Perfect again. Cut!

I turn around, and the ad guy is heading my way. He's not happy. He tells me that Mickey is still rushing. I stand up, throw my hands in the air, point to the chimp and say, "You talk to him. He won't listen to me!'"

TWELVE
AUDITIONS (AND OTHER HORROR STORIES)

Sometimes an audition is fun. After a short time in the film business, an actor becomes typecast. When a writer/ producer contacts a casting office to set up auditions for a project, the casting people are provided with information as to age, ethnicity, weight, and height, avuncular or grumpy, etc. As a result, many times you will find yourself in a casting office with actors you see often, who are in your general category or type, and are up for the same part. This is particularly true where commercials are concerned. While we are all waiting in the outer office to be seen by the producers, we swap stories, tell jokes, and lie about how busy we've been to pass the time and ease the tension. Seeing these old faces and sizing them up brings a certain validation and comfort in knowing you are in the right place and in the proper wardrobe.

Occasionally, however, they will cast against type. For instance, if the role is for a murderer on a detective show, they may decide to cast someone who hasn't had a career playing bad guys, so as not to give away the ending. Sometimes they will be unsure or undecided and you will be informed they are seeing all types. Here are a few stories that happened in casting offices:

I was called in to play Hope's father on a show called *Hope and Gloria*. When I arrived at the casting office at Warner Brothers in Burbank, I could immediately see that something was amiss. Most of the guys were at least ten years older than me, and they all were dressed like bank presidents. I must have received the wrong information from my agent, or, more likely, the person who gave me said information was an incompetent boob. I was told the dress was casual, and I looked like I had just come off the golf course, which was accurate. *Oh well*, I thought. *Que sera, sera.*

I didn't know most of the guys, but I saw Richard Herd, who played my boss in *The China Syndrome*. Richard was an excellent actor who is always unflappable. I hoped he wasn't up for the father role. If he was,

My favorite headshot. *Author Collection.*

I was sunk. I signed in on the SAG talent sheet and found a chair next to his. He looked cool, confident, and prepared.

"Hey, Richard. What's up?"

He looked up from his script.

"Not much. Pilot for *Disney*. Couple of MOWs. You?"

Damn! A working actor always has an edge over one who is currently at liberty. I hadn't worked in months. The people who hire will know. I will smell like carrion.

"About the same. Got a recurring role on *Melrose Place*. Waiting to hear about a feature with Burt."

All of which was total crap, of course. I hoped he and all the others were up for another part. Not the father. *Oh please, not the father.*

I tried to sound polite but bored. "Which role are you reading for?"

"There is only one . . . the father. May be recurring. You?"

I smiled sweetly as I picked up a copy of *Variety*. I was stalling.

"I'm up for the golf pro at the country club. Great role."

When I'm cornered, I'm dangerous. Richard began shuffling through his script.

"Golf pro? Country club? I don't . . . "

"Didn't you get the rewrite? Oh yeah. Big scene at the country club when Biff, the tipsy golf pro, runs the golf cart into the ice sculpture, which falls into the wedding cake, and he says, 'May I play through?' It's hilarious. Great role. They sent the script out to the house. You didn't get the rewrites?"

"Now, why didn't my agent tell me all this? I play golf! Damned incompetent boob!"

He shoots . . . he scores! Dick is definitely flappable. The casting director came around the corner from her inner office as Bank President Number Nineteen was leaving.

"Mr. Herd? We're ready for you."

Richard was still muttering about his agent when he went in. I gave him the thumbs-up. He was toast. Five minutes later we nodded as I went in. There were about six people in the office; executive producer, director, writers, and casting lady. I was the last guy they were seeing. It had been a long casting session, and they looked tired. I sat down in the empty chair facing them, leaned back and said, "Gentlemen, I am what is known as . . . another way to go!"

Fortunately, everyone thought that was funny as hell, and I got the part.

I am not ashamed to say there were a few little tricks I employed over the years to increase the odds of getting a part in my favor. I have no way of knowing if any of these little gimmicks really worked, but they didn't hurt my self-confidence and sense of fun.

Back in the Ice Age, when I started working in Hollywood, every actor came to a casting session with a picture. It was a black-and-white eight-by-ten-inch headshot. As I had been a photographer for a few years, I knew something many people didn't. After the photograph has been printed and washed, it is placed on a large, heated metal revolving drum, emulsion side down. This made the surface glossy as it dried. It also imparted a slight upward curve on the print. Now the fun comes in. If you have a stack of these photos, the curvature is more pronounced. If you curve the photo with your hands in the opposite direction, like a sheet off a paper-towel roll, it will pop up slightly, separating it from the rest of the pile. So, if someone just grabs a bunch of photos off a stack, my photo would be the one left on top.

In every casting office there is a Screen Actors Guild sign-in sheet. You sign your name and social security number and a few other bits of information. Occasionally, I would simply draw a star by my name or a series of exclamation points, as though someone thought this person was pretty special. I don't know if the casting people or the clients ever looked at these sheets to refresh their memories, but if they did, I'll bet they included my name among those who were submitted for the callback.

Just for fun, when the outer office was filled with applicants for the job, I would back in from the hallway while I pretended to be talking to someone involved with the shooting of the commercial. Something like this:

"Thursday? Yes, I'm available. Well thank you, that's very nice of you. My sizes? Thirty waist, thirty-one inseam, fifteen-and-a-half shirt."

Well, you get the idea.

Finally, here is something just for actors who might be reading this. It isn't a trick, it's an attitude. Don't go in there with your hat in your hand expecting not to be hired. Don't even think about how much you want and or need this job. You get more jobs when you don't need them than when you do. Think of it this way: everybody in that room has a problem. They need to find someone for that part. You are going to help them solve that problem. You are the answer. They need you, not the other way around. Be the best you that you can be. And don't be afraid to be funny and charming. You may not be exactly what they want for the project, but if they remember you, you might be perfect the next time you meet.

Many times I heard a director or producer ask me just before we read, "Do you have any questions?"

I often answered, "Just one. Is it all right to beg?"

I went up for a nice guest star part on *Barnaby Jones* once and everything went great. I was told to wait outside while they made a decision. It's always good news when they ask you to wait. After a few minutes, the associate producer

Rascal me. *Author Collection.*

Backward dance in high school—I'm the one in the dress.
Author Collection.

stuck his head out the door and asked me if I knew my dress size. Naturally, I thought he was kidding and made a flippant remark. But he was serious. Thinking quickly, I told him I thought I was about a size twelve. He looked dismayed and ducked back into the conference room. A few minutes later I was dismissed.

Later I learned that the episode involved a man who commits a murder wearing a dress, thereby being mistakenly identified as a woman. The sequence had already been shot with a stunt double who wore a size ten.

I have lost parts because I was too young, too old, too tall, too short, or too skinny, but this was the only time I lost a job because I couldn't squeeze into a size ten.

Hollywood can be like a small town—the gossip can make you or break you. It has always been a buyer's market in show business. For every part, there are dozens of capable, talented actors who are eager to further their careers. One thing every actor must learn to deal with is rejection. If you are thin-skinned and sensitive, you might want to investigate an alternative career choice. After all, most of the time and through no fault of your own, you won't get the job. Let me describe a casting interview that more or less honest to God probably happened more than once.

My agent calls me the night before an audition and gives me all the pertinent information. My appointment is at 2:00 p.m. the next day. The part is for a possibly recurring guest-star role on a top-rated comedy television show. I will be reading for the producer and the multi-Emmy-winning director. The dress is upscale casual. My agent has a good feeling about this one. Soon my fax machine prints out my sides and as I read them, I begin to laugh out loud. The script is brilliant, and I really am perfect for the part. I commit the scene to memory and get to bed early to be well rested for the next day.

The freeway was practically empty, and I arrive fifteen minutes early at the studio gate. After the guard confirms my name on his clipboard, he directs me to a parking space near the building where the show is officed. I enter the building, impressed by the black-leather-and-chrome lobby furniture as I approach the security desk and sign in. A courteous uniformed security officer directs me down a hallway filled with cast pictures of previous and current hit shows. I can't help imagining my own picture up there.

I reach the outer office of the show and am greeted by a vivacious young woman who asks me if I would like something to drink. I sign in on the SAG sheet and see that there is only one other actor ahead of me. The cheerful brunette brings me a cold bottle of designer water as I relax in a comfortable chair and tells me it won't be but a minute. I'm not sure . . . was she flirting with me? Probably just a fan. Within minutes, the actor who was ahead of me smiles and nods at me on his way out. It's my turn now. The flirtatious receptionist ushers me into the producer's sumptuous office, which is tastefully overdone. The casting lady introduces me to the writer-producer-creator-show runner and the director, who all tell me how much they enjoy my work. They ask, "What was it like to work with Burt/Jim/Jane/Jack or Doris?" And, "Are the rumors true about Forrest Tucker's whang-doodle?"

Everyone is very jovial, and the director says there is no need for me to read. He knows that I could do this role standing on my head. Everyone nods in agreement, and I'm asked if I'm free the following week.

"Well, I'm not free but I am reasonable," I say.

I exit to peals of laughter and knowing nods. On the way home, I stop at a pay phone and call my agent to tell him to hold out for big dough because this one is in the bag. I absolutely nailed it. It has been a perfect day.

I call my agent about twenty times over the next three days until he finally tells me they went another way. I feel crushed and betrayed, but I must get on with my life and put all this behind me. A couple of months later, I am surfing the tube and hear a snippet of familiar dialogue, so I pause long enough to see an overweight Spanish lady doing the part I was up for. She's terrible. The canned laughter was obvious. I would kick the cat at this point, but I don't have one. What a loser. I can't even afford a cat.

Agents have a tough job. Actors always want to know why we didn't get the part. After being on both sides of the camera, I now know that there are myriad reasons for picking one actor over another. But as actors, we believe we must have done something wrong, or forgotten to do something right, which caused us to lose the part. This is rarely the case. Sometimes they want a special look, some indefinable something that they feel they will recognize when they see it. Sometimes a part is lost because a network executive tells the producer that the network is interested in an actor who is in a hit Broadway show.

There are many reasons not to get hired but only a few that will actually get you the job. If it works out, you almost always hear the good news right away. In the entertainment industry, no news is usually bad news. In any case, no one from the production office

ever calls all the agents who represent the actors that weren't hired to explain why they didn't measure up. And if they did, no agent would be cruel enough to pass on the information.

"Hello, is this the Goliath Talent Agency?"

"Yes it is. This is Leo Gortch speaking, and you are . . .?"

"I'm calling from the *Fiddle DeeDee* show. You have a client you submitted to us."

"I did? To tell you the truth I had no idea. I send out so many pictures. Who is the lucky actor?"

"His name is Neville Swarthmore."

"Neville! Of course. A great actor. I found him at a dinner theater in Del Mar. So . . . what are we talking? Top of the show or scale plus ten?"

"Neither. We didn't hire him."

"So why the call? I don't understand."

"We just wanted you to know your client is a talentless hack."

"Really? Maybe he was nervous . . ."

"Nervous schmervous, your client stunk on ice. He shouldn't be allowed to breed. After his audition, we had to fumigate the office. Just thought you ought to know."

"Thanks anyway, I got another call. Goliath . . ."

"Leo? Neville here. Have you heard from *Fiddle DeeDee*? I thought I really nailed the audition! Any word?"

"Sorry, Neville. They loved what you did, but they went another way."

There are at least two phrases every agent has to learn:

1. They went another way.

2. It's down to you and another guy.

At least Larry Kubik, my agent for many years, always let me down gently. When I called the first time, I would get, "It's between you and another guy." See, now that brought hope. They had narrowed the field down to two players and I'm still in the running! Out of all the guys who were at the audition, I now have a fifty-fifty chance.

Then, when I called the next day I would get, "They went another way." He always said it in a really disgusted tone like, "Can you believe those idiots?"

God bless Larry and all the other agents who were always there with an umbrella when it rained on my parade.

There is an old joke in Hollywood about the actor whose agent called to tell him to get out to the Rose Bowl as they are about to make a picture with a gigantic cast and they are seeing all types. The actor goes to the Rose Bowl and there are thousands of actors waiting in line. The actor gets in line for four hours and eventually they put him on videotape. The next day he calls his agent.

"How'd I do?"

"How'd you do what?"

"How'd I do at the audition? You know the one where they saw all types?"

"Oh . . .They went another way."

Occasionally (make that rarely), I seem to get the part no matter what. Occasionally (make that often), I can, for no plausible reason, really get pretty negative when it comes to my career. I don't know why it is, but if there is any little thing that seems to indicate that the part wasn't necessarily written with me in mind, I start a downward spiral in my head. I think I try to prepare myself for failure by trying to think of all the reasons why I am not about to get the next thing that comes my way. I drive family members, managers, and agents absolutely nuts.

Some years ago, there was a wonderful comedy called *Full House.* The stars were Bob Saget, John Stamos, Dave Coulier, and the Olsen twins, among others. They were looking for a boss for Dave and John. There was no information regarding the role apart from the name of the character, Mr. Malatesta. Right away I knew I would never get the part.

Mr. Malatesta had (in my opinion) an Italian sound. Franco Malatesta or Giuseppe Malatesta sounded about right, I thought. What producer in their right mind would hire me for that role? So, right away, I began to sink into the sea of despair.

There was more bad news. The audition time was set for 6:00 p.m. That was right in the heart of the LA evening traffic. Of course, there is no time that the LA freeways aren't busy, but from 4:00 p.m. until around 8:00 p.m., it's a creeping-along-a-few-feet-at-a-time parking lot. And that is only if the weather is good and there are no accidents or police chases.

The address of the audition was in Culver City. That translates to about thirty miles of aforementioned creeping on the 405. It was almost 4:00 p.m. I'd have to get a move on. I knew a way over the canyon that was actually longer but usually quicker. Just about then, it started raining. When it finally does rain in LA, it isn't like anything you have ever seen anywhere else. It is a cataclysmic, end-of-the-world, is-that-a-house-sliding-down-that-hill, kind of rain. If you are driving in it, it seems as if you are

underwater, and if you live in the Valley, then very often you are. Nevertheless, I made it to MGM with a few minutes to spare. I saw a few of my buddies looking as forlorn as I was feeling and just as wet. There was a sign-in sheet and sides to read but no receptionist or casting person to give us a clue as to what the producers were looking for. Every physical and ethnic type and age range was represented in that room.

Soon my name was called. I went in and read and was thanked and politely dismissed. *Well, that's that,* I thought.

I got home around 8:00 p.m. There was a message from my agent. I called him up to give him an earful.

"Why was I submitted for this role? I was so wrong for the part. It was humiliating."

My agent told me he had been informed that it was between me and Marcia Wallace. I was too stunned to react when I was told they had left for a dinner break but would resume casting at 9:00 p.m.

I did get the role and subsequently did three episodes as well as two or three episodes of other shows the producers had on the air. I always felt I should have apologized to Marcia for getting the part. I know she would have made a terrific Mr. Malatesta.

I probably sign more autographed photos from *Teen Wolf* than I do from any other movie or television show I've done except *F Troop.* No one has been more surprised than me. Apparently, the role of Michael J. Fox's father, Harold Howard, is one of my most recognizable roles. The funny thing is, I didn't originally audition for that part. I auditioned for the role of the coach in the film (which was, incidentally, played flawlessly by Jay Tarses).

I went into the studio to read for the part and was feeling pretty good about it when I left. When I finished, I said goodbye to the casting director and headed down the hall. Moments later, I heard the casting director calling out after me. Would I, she asked, be willing to come back and read for another role? Crap. That meant I had probably blown it. No fun coach role for me.

As I slouched down the hall back to the casting room, I felt like a dismal failure. I wondered, as most middle-aged actors do at times, if I had become a washed-up old hack. How would I feed my family? How would I face my friends? Would my agent fire me? I would probably be reading for Guy Number 3 or Paramedic Number 2.

But it was not meant to be. Michael had seen my first audition minutes earlier and had asked the casting director if they had cast the role of his father yet. They had not. That's when, the casting director later told me, she ran down the hall to retrieve me. Michael and I read together and the chemistry was, well, undeniable. I was his dad and he was my son. It was a little movie that was better than it had to be. And Michael? He was the best. He was and is such a hard-working actor. Everyone knows the story of how he was plucked from our picture to work on *Back to the Future*. He was literally working day and night. Ah, youth!

I have been asked many times how long I had to sit in the makeup chair to "wolf out" for my role. It was around four hours, but that was just for my face and hands. Poor Michael had to endure a much longer trial of sitting and itching in order to cover his entire body. Now ask me how long it took to take it off. Less than thirty seconds. I would begin ripping and pulling at my face the instant the director said "Cut" at the end of my last scene for the day. I'm terribly claustrophobic.

Teen Wolf fans are amazing. Some of them can quote entire scenes, playing multiple characters. If you've seen the movie, you'll probably agree that my most memorable scene occurs in a bathroom doorway. After much protest, Michael's character, Scott, who has just "wolfed out," concedes to opening the door to his father who, to everyone's surprise, is also a werewolf. My line at that point is "An explanation is probably long overdue." The only other line I remember saying is "That went well." The reason I recall that line specifically is because the scene had ended with Michael's character stomping off, leaving me sitting alone at a table with a cup of coffee. The director, Rod Daniel, forgot to say "Cut" and I ad-libbed while the cameras continued to roll for a minute. Since then I've heard that phrase uttered in a plethora of films and television shows. I've often wondered if *Teen Wolf* actually kick-started that expression.

Another quick piece of trivia involves a scene between my character and the character of Rusty Thorne, the school's vice principal (my pal Jim MacKrell). Thorne

Two werewolves: David Naughton, star of *An American Werewolf in London,* and me. *Author Collection.*

gives Michael's character, Scott, a hard time throughout the film. When asked why, I tell Scott about a confrontation that occurred between us years earlier where things certainly did not go Thorne's way. So, when it came time to film the scene where my character walks in on Thorne threatening Scott, Jim and I felt that we needed to find a way for Rusty to be reminded of what had happened the

Wolfing out on the set of *Teen Wolf.* *Author Collection.*

More makeup! *Author Collection.*

Taking the wolf off at last! *Author Collection.*

(Top) An incredible "Wolfed Out" *Teen Wolf* fan. (Middle) With the talented Jason Bateman. (Bottom) New *Teen Wolf* dunks. *Author Collection.*

last time he got crosswise with Harold. We spoke to the director about it and he told us we could add something but was adamant that it had to be quick. No more than thirty seconds. The little scene by the lockers where the principal loses control of his "bodily functions" made it into the picture. Gold!

Even though *Teen Wolf* was filmed prior to *Back to the Future*, since the latter was a bigger budget picture, they released it first in hopes that *Teen Wolf* would get a kick-start. It worked. I have been so touched by the many fans who have told me how my character reminded them of their own father or how they wished they would have had a father like my character. Nowadays, kids who watched that movie in the theaters are watching it with their own kids on cable, and still enjoying it. Makes me feel really good.

I reprised my role as Harold Howard in the sequel, *Teen Wolf Too,* with Jason Bateman playing my nephew. What a talented kid. *Teen Wolf Too* was Jason's first film role and his father happened to be producing. Unfortunately, Jason's parents were going through a divorce, and it was a fairly difficult time for him. You'd never guess it from his performance and his professionalism on the set. He had great comedy chops (no pun intended). I can't remember whether we had already worked together on *The Hogan Family* or not, but we were natural pals. He, too, has gone on to become a big star. Well deserved.

This leads me to another related audition story. My agent called to say that there was going to be a Saturday morning cartoon version of *Teen Wolf,* and the cartoon character of Harold Howard looked just like me. Eureka! I love doing voice-overs. You can go to the studio in your pajamas, without brushing your teeth or putting on deodorant, and no one is the wiser! There was just one catch—I had to audition. What? Are you kidding me? I had just played the role of Harold Howard in both of the *Teen Wolf* films! In fact, I was the only actor who would be working on the cartoon version of the movie who was part of the original cast. Yet the network was insisting that I audition. What gall! How rude! The nerve! Of course, I hightailed it down to the studio to read. I booked it. When it aired, the cartoon-character version of Harold Howard looked nothing like me. No way was I that rotund. Typical Hollywood.

On the set of *Teen Wolf Too. Author Collection.*

Teen Wolf Brand Chili Layered Salad

INGREDIENTS

1 15-ounce can of Wolf Brand Chili
1 can ranch style beans
2 Roma tomatoes, chopped
½ cup chopped black olives
½ small red onion, chopped
Guacamole (Try to make your own!)
4 cups iceberg lettuce
1 cup shredded Colby Jack cheese
2 cups Fritos Corn Chips (Mother Nature's perfect food)

DIRECTIONS

Heat chili and ranch style beans in separate saucepans. Layer chili and then beans in the bottom of a two-quart glass bowl. Layer tomatoes, black olives, onion, guacamole, lettuce, and cheese on top of the beans. Top with Fritos and serve immediately. Ahh-wooooooo!

THIRTEEN
FAMILIAR FACES

I used to get a little miffed when I heard myself referred to as a character actor. I wanted to be known simply as an *actor*, and hopefully a good one. Period. The expression "character actor" seemed redundant to me. After all, don't all actors play characters? Still, not everybody is a star.

What I think is that the term *character actor,* in most people's minds, seems to mean someone they recognize, but they can't remember their names. There are a lot of us that fall into that category. We are the actors who don't get the girl (or guy), and we get killed off a lot. I got killed in the film *Soldier Blue* before the opening credits were over.

It's comparatively easy to remember the stars. Their names are plastered all over the screen at the beginning of the movie and the letters are ten feet tall. The names of the actors playing the supporting roles come at the end of the film while the ushers are cleaning up the popcorn. So what have we got here? We have movie stars, and then we

(Top) Me and my moustache in *Soldier Blue.* (Middle) With the amazing Barry Corbin. (Bottom) With the lovely Leslie Easterbrook, my costar on *Police Academy V.* (Left) With my buddy Bernie Kopell—Ahoy! *Author Collection.*

Cigar aficionados Jack McGee and me. *Author Collection.*

With my golfing buddy and actor extraordinaire Jonathan Banks. *Author Collection.*

With the oh so talented Andrew Prine. *Author Collection.*

With friend Glenn Morshower. *Author Collection.*

have perfectly good actors who make a nice living without making the cover of the *National Enquirer.*

I tried to explain all this to a guy once and he brightened right up and said, "Oh, I get it. You're a bit player!"

Nowadays I find I am quite agreeable to be included in the group we call character actors, and what a group of characters they are. Below, in no particular order, are a few I have had the pleasure to know and was proud to work with.

STROTHER MARTIN (STORY #1)

I first met Strother on the set of *The Doris Day Show*. I was amazed at how a charming, well-educated raconteur, who had once been a world-ranked springboard diver, could transform himself into an unkempt, shiftless, whiskey-swilling con man. He also possessed the most amazing memory. When I mentioned how much I enjoyed his performances in *Cool Hand Luke*, *Butch Cassidy and the Sundance Kid,* and *The Man Who Shot Liberty Valance*, he was able to recite whole scenes. He told me that once he committed something to memory, he never forgot it.

There are a lot of great stories about Strother. Denver Pyle told me one about the time he was directing

As William Randolph Hearst on *Death Valley Days.* *Author Collection.*

Strother on an episode of *Death Valley Days*. I had also appeared on the show once as William Randolph Hurst. They were shooting in the desert outside of Tucson. The temperature was in triple digits, and as always seems the case, the company was getting behind. Strother was playing a character named Death Valley Scotty. Scotty was an old prospector who, as the story goes, had located a secret silver mine somewhere in the Superstition Mountains. Scotty would go off alone with only his mule and return a few days later with bags of silver. The wardrobe Strother had to wear included long johns, a long-sleeved wool shirt, leather leggings and moccasins, patched and tattered wool pants, a floppy hat, and a big bearskin coat. This was before actors had air-conditioned trailers a few steps away complete with a refrigerator full of ice-cold beverages. All an actor could expect back then was a canvas set chair near the honey wagon.

Several times when Denver asked the first assistant director to find Strother, he would be stripped to his skivvies in the shade of a saguaro cactus. When Denver argued it was costing the company time for him to get re-dressed for the scene, Strother would reply, "But Denver it's too hot!" It became his mantra that day. No matter how Denver pleaded and cajoled, the response was the same, "But it's too hot, Denver. It's just too damn hot!"

Finally, they had gotten all the shots with Strother except for the most important one, the opening. Denver envisioned a long shot of Scotty emerging from behind the rocks high up the trail, with the sun setting in the background behind him and his faithful mule. Denver patiently described the shot to Strother.

"All right Strother, here's the deal. You see that spot up that mountain where those two rocks are by that big cactus?"

Strother nodded.

Denver continued, "Take the mule and plenty of water and go up there. Find a shady spot and relax. We've got a couple more scenes to do and then we're going to do the opening shot. Scotty, fully clothed, riding down that trail out of the mountains on his mule. You just keep on coming all the way down and past the camera, and that's a cut. Later we will edit in the Old Ranger's narration. Now listen closely Strother, we only have one try at this, so be ready to come when I yell 'Action.' Can you do that?"

"Of course I can do that, Denver. It's just that it's so damn hot."

Off they went, Strother and the mule, while the rest of the cast and crew worked feverishly to complete the

With Lori Patrick on *Death Valley Days*, 1965. *Author Collection.*

Horsing around on *Death Valley Days* with Robert Cornthwaite—don't you love that name? *Author Collection.*

day's shooting. For once, everything went smoothly, and they were able to shoot the remaining two scenes and get the coverage that was needed. At last it was time for the opening shot. The camera crew swung the camera into position as the sun was setting beautifully. The director of photography squinted at the sun, checked his light meter and nodded to his director.

Denver picked up his bullhorn. "All right Strother, we are ready to go. Mount up and when I say 'Action,' come out from behind those rocks. Have you got that?"

"I got it," came the small voice through the desert stillness.

"All right, roll camera. Speed. Action!"

Nothing.

"Action, Strother!"

Still nothing.

"Goddammit Strother! If you and that mule don't come out of there, I'm going to kill you both! We are losing the light. Now action!"

A pause, then, "I can't come out."

"Why the hell not?"

"The mule has fainted! I told you. It's too damn hot!"

Sure enough, when they reached Strother, the mule that he had left standing in the sun (while he was relaxing in the shade) had suffered a sunstroke and was passed out cold.

STROTHER MARTIN (STORY #2)

My favorite Strother Martin story took place on the set of the television show *Hawkins on Murder*. Jimmy Stewart was the star of this series filmed at MGM. It was more than a nod to the wonderful film *Anatomy of a Murder*, which also starred Stewart, with Lee Remick, Ben Gazzara, and Arthur O'Connell. Strother played a role similar to the one O'Connell played in the movie. Strother, as Jimmy's assistant and brother, was a wonderful foil against Jimmy's quiet, thoughtful defense lawyer.

Jimmy had his dressing-room trailer nearby, but he preferred to join the rest of the cast while we waited for the gaffers and grips to light the scene. We relaxed in our canvas set chairs with our names on the back that the prop department provided. They were always neatly placed close to the set but out of the way of the work. Sometimes we would rehearse a little, but usually we'd grab a smoke, swap stories, or read the trades.

Jimmy was an incurable practical joker and loved to yank Strother's political chain. Strother, an avid liberal Democrat, would always rise to the bait when Jimmy, a moderate Republican, would make supportive remarks concerning President Nixon. It was all in fun for Jimmy and very entertaining for the rest of us, but not for Strother. Strother equated Richard Nixon to the Antichrist and refused to see any good in the man. One day while we were enjoying the banter between the two, Jimmy winked at me and dropped his bomb.

"You know Strother, you'll have to admit Nixon has done a lot for the economy."

Time stood still. All work stopped. The gauntlet had been thrown. Strother, always respectful to Jimmy, slowly rose out of his chair with a look of complete incredulity on his face. He seemed to be having some trouble breathing. He began to pace back and forth, running his hands through his hair. Then, he exploded.

"Goddammit Jimmy! Nixon has done for the economy what pantyhose has done for foreplay!"

PAT BUTTRAM

Pat Buttram was one of the wittiest humans who ever lived. The crackly voiced actor was Gene Autry's sidekick for many successful years before his role as Mr. Haney on *Green Acres*. His acerbic and surprisingly sophisticated wit made him one of Hollywood's favorite toastmasters. His deadpan delivery of the punch line always caught us off guard. I believe, although I can't prove it, that he is the source of the following story.

"Did y'all hear about Pia Zadora doin' that play in Orange County? Aw yeah, she wanted to prove that she was a dramatic actress, so she starred in *The Diary of Anne Frank*. Didn't work out too well, though. On opening night when the storm troopers came to search the house, the whole audience stood up and yelled, 'She's in the attic! She's in the attic!'"

Pat was successful at everything he did, but he got his start in radio where his distinctive voice was an asset. It almost had a little yodel in it, not unlike a teenager whose voice is changing. To my delight, we occasionally found ourselves paired in comedic radio commercials. His Alabama accent and my Texas twang worked well together. We were making just such a commercial at

Waves, a company that specialized in amusing radio ads. We had finished the commercial and the producer was satisfied, but we were asked to wait while they called the sponsor to make sure he was happy with it. Just to kill a little time, I thought I'd ask him about his relationship with cowboy star Gene Autry, or Gene "Artery" as Pat called him. I had heard a story or two about Gene enjoying an occasional libation.

"Oh yeah, me and Gene used to have a drop or two from time to time. You know, just to wind down. One night I was out in the Valley looking for him, but I couldn't find him anywhere. I tried every watering hole on Ventura Boulevard. Nobody had seen him. It was getting late, and I was starting to get worried. Finally, I stopped into the bar at the Sportsmen's Lodge. I went up to the bartender and said, 'Have you seen Gene?' The bartender said, 'You're a'standin' on him.'"

Old cowboys (and a cowgirl). Front row: Ken Farmer, Roberta Shore, Alex Cord. Second row: James Drury, Paul Petersen, Charlie LeSueur, Buck Stienke. Back row: Robert Fuller, me, Michael McGreevey, Michael Dante. *Author Collection.*

GUICH KOOCK

I worked with Guich on at least two occasions. We were both cast in Roy Rogers's last movie, *Mackintosh and T.J.*, and Guich was a regular on Suzanne Somers's show *She's the Sheriff*.

Guich was from a small town in Texas named Luckenbach, the same one the song is about. He was great company during many long hours of filming on location in West Texas. Once I asked Guich how he came to have such an unusual name.

"Well, my daddy raised dogs, don't you know?"

He stopped there as if that was all the information needed.

"Yes, okay, your daddy raised dogs. Is that it?"

"Well, the dogs got all the good names."

One of my favorite stories is one about Guich and a friend of his who decided to have a nice dinner at a fine restaurant in Austin. His friend ordered roast chicken. When it arrived, he cut into the chicken and pink water began to seep out. Realizing that it had not been properly cooked, he took a novel approach to a problem all of us have had from time to time when we have been presented with a food order not to our satisfaction. We are hungry and we don't want to wait for the soup to be warmed, or perhaps our hamburger is well done instead of rare, as we requested. Usually, we meekly pick at our food and wish we could stand up for ourselves and object to this sort of incompetence. Above all, we don't want to make a scene. Well, this Texan had no problem with expressing his displeasure. He picked up the undercooked fowl, hurled it in the direction of the kitchen and shouted, "Fly you summbitch! You ain't hurt that bad!"

EDGAR BUCHANAN

I was playing golf with Edgar Buchanan at one of the Hollywood Hacker tournaments. We had just driven off the tee and we were walking down the fairway. Buck turned to me and in his distinctive gravelly voice said:

"Say Jim, do you know the definition of a bogey?"

"No, I don't think I do, Buck."

"It's two 'oh nos,' two 'oh shits,' and a forty-foot putt."

Always time for a round of golf. *Author Collection.*

HEDLEY MATTINGLY

Hedley was another golfing pal from the Hollywood Hackers. For many years he was one of the best friends I had, and we played countless games of golf. He was a greatly accomplished actor and will be remembered for his role as the game warden on the television show *Daktari*.

Hedley was the epitome of British stiff-upper-lip-ness. When the doctor informed him and his wife, Barbara, that he had inoperable cancer and only a short time left on earth, he replied:

"Well, thank you Doctor, but I cannot tell you how disappointed I am to hear that."

I remember a time when we were playing golf at a county course in the San Fernando Valley. On the third hole, we saw some boys from the local lockup in orange coveralls cutting weeds and cleaning up trash around the course. They seemed to be showing an inordinate amount of interest in our group. In fact, they seemed to be following us. After my tee shot on the fourth hole, I noticed they had crept up a little closer. I turned around and asked them what they were doing there. They told me they were in a county youth detention program. They were so excited to meet me. I was puzzled. Then it all became clear. They knew me from a movie that I had starred in called *Hawmps!* about camels in the cavalry before the Civil War. They told me that *Hawmps!* was the only movie they had on tape and they watched it two or three times a week.

I told them to contact their lawyers and tell them that making them watch that movie was cruel and unusual punishment.

Me in my old *Hawmps!* uniform. *Courtesy of Joe Camp.*

BOB DONNER (STORY #1)

About twenty-five years ago or so, I was visiting someone in an Encino hospital. On my way out I ran into a distraught Cissy (then Bob's wife) who told me Bob had had a heart attack and was in intensive care. I asked if I could see him, but she told me only family members were allowed. When she left, I went to the nurses' station and told them I was Bob's brother from Cleveland. I was granted five minutes.

When I entered his room, he looked like he was sleeping, so I just stood quietly and took in the scene. He was plugged into all kinds of machines. There were tubes all over the place, including one that had these sort of radar-looking blips monitoring his heartbeat. I just

With my good friend Bob Donner. *Author Collection.*

wanted to see him and say a little prayer. As I was about to leave, he began to stir and opened his eyes.

Gradually he recognized me, took a beat, and said:

"Well Hamp, it looks like forty-compression balls from here on out."

60

We both started to laugh and Bob started shaking. Blips started blipping and EKG's were ringing alarms somewhere, which only made us howl with more laughter. We couldn't stop.

As irate doctors and nurses were escorting me out, I wondered how many guys I knew that could make a joke that good under those circumstances. The answer is just Bob.

BOB DONNER (STORY #2)

Donner and I were teeing it up at Braemar Golf Course. We had played a couple of holes and Bob seemed unusually quiet. Finally, I asked what was eating him. He told me that his agent had called the day before and *Gunsmoke* had offered him a role. He didn't have to audition as he had already done two episodes of *Gunsmoke*, and they knew his work. It was a firm offer with top of the show money.

I said, "Great! So, what's the problem?"

He said he had just received the script that morning, and when he skimmed through it with great anticipation, he was shocked.

"Three lines, Hamp! Three lines! How could they do that? I'm no bit player for Chrissakes! How could they do that?"

I was very sympathetic and supportive with my old friend. How could they do that indeed? I shook my head. What was there to say? We played a few more holes and Bob poured his heart out. It wasn't an ego thing. It was about respect. Respect that he had earned through hard work. Bob had paid his dues.

Finally, we reached the little snack shack before the turn.

"You know what I feel like doing, Hamp? I feel like telling them to take their little three-line part and shove it!"

I told him I didn't blame him. I told him I wished I had the courage to draw a line in the sand and strike a blow for all actors. I was in complete agreement with his stance. It was like a cloud had lifted from him. He asked if I minded if he went ahead and putted out. He shook my hand and told me how much he appreciated being able to get this weight off his chest. He thanked me for being so understanding and decided not to stew over this any longer. I lent him a quarter for the pay phone in the snack shack so he could call his agent. He almost sprinted off the green.

He was on the phone talking to his agent's secretary and was being told the agent would have to call him back.

"Well, would you mind telling him this is very important to me and I need to talk to him right away?"

Fantastic Hill Street Blues Golf Tournament Players. Look for Peter Marshall, Ivan Dixon, Alex Trebek, Dennis Franz, Charles Haid, Betty Thomas, Matthew Lawrence, Rick Hurst, Ed Nelson, George "Spanky" McFarland, Bruce Weitz, Craig T. Nelson, Arte Johnson, Powers Booth, and Alvy Moore, among others. *Author Collection.*

Golf with the boys: Sam McMurray, Jonathan Banks, and Tom Parks. *Author Collection.*

He was boiling as he slammed down the receiver. I asked him if I could use the phone.

"Well, gee Hamp, I'm waiting to hear from my agent!"

"I know," I replied. "This won't take a second."

I dropped in a quarter and pretended to dial as Bob paced.

"Hi. Yeah, everything is all right. I just need a favor. Would you call my agent and tell him there is going to be a part available on *Gunsmoke* in about five minutes? Thanks, bye."

It took about three incredulous beats before he realized he had been had. He roared with laughter. He laughed so hard he could hardly stand. The phone rang. It was his agent. Bob couldn't talk. He could barely breathe.

"What do you want me to tell him?"

"Tell him . . . never mind."

JACK WARDEN

The wonderful Jack Warden told this story when we were working on *The Man Who Loved Cat Dancing*. We were in Gila Bend, Arizona, at the time. Jack was a master storyteller and a delightful drinking companion.

I was in New York working on *Twelve Angry Men*. After shooting all day, I flagged a cab and headed for the Village for some pizza. I could see the cabbie looking into his rearview mirror with that sort of "where do I know you from?" look on his face. Finally, he snapped his fingers.

"I know you! You're that actor, right?"

I nodded.

"Sure, I know you. You been in lots of stuff. What's your name?"

"It's Jack Warden."

"Imagine that! Jack Warden in my cab! How about that?"

I tried to be modest, but he was effusive.

"Say you must know a lot of beautiful actresses, huh?"

"Well, I know a few, I guess."

"Natalie Wood! Now there's a real beauty. You know Natalie Wood?"

"No . . . to tell the truth, I've never had the pleasure."

"She's somethin' boy, that Natalie Wood. How about Piper Laurie? You know Piper Laurie?"

I wanted to help him out as he seemed so eager, but I couldn't.

"Well of course I'm a big fan of hers, but we've never actually met."

The cabbie was eyeing me and looking a little disappointed, but I could see he was going to give it one more try.

"How about Eva Marie Saint? You ever met Eva Marie Saint?"

Jackpot! I had met her. I couldn't wait to share the news and regain the respect I had lost by not knowing Natalie and Piper.

"Well you know, it's a funny thing. I was just at a party a couple of weeks ago and she was there. We talked about doing a play together. Oh yeah, I know Eva Marie all right."

This seemed to cheer him right up. He looked in the mirror at me in a conspiratorial way.

"No kidding? Well, me and you have something in common, Jack."

"Really? What's that? Has she been in your cab?"

"Nah! Better than that. I shtupped her maid!"

FOURTEEN
ASSIGNMENT: F TROOP

F Troop is, without a doubt, one of the funniest shows ever produced. If I wanted to, I could write an entire book on this wonderful show that only lasted two years. I cannot overemphasize the importance of it in my life. The best place to begin is how I got to be a part of that incredible bunch of gifted, creative, and dedicated people who would generously teach me the dos and don'ts of filmed entertainment.

It was late fall in 1965 and I had just finished my third *Gunsmoke*. It wasn't the character of Jeb that I had played twice before; it was a new character named Eliab. On Friday, we completed the episode titled "Eliab's Aim," and I was invited to join the cast and crew for a drink or two. The Friday wrap party on *Gunsmoke* was famous. If you wished to take part, you clipped a buck or two to a clever little money tree made by the prop department. It was a bare bush full of clothespins that, at the end of Friday's shoot, was filled with folded money. The prop man then took the "leaves" off the tree and bought booze. As soon as the assistant director announced, "Ladies and gentlemen, that's a wrap," the bar was open.

It was very convivial and jolly, and I received quite a few pats on the back for my performance. I was having a few drinks when our director Richard Sarafian kindly offered to buy me dinner. It's a funny thing about actors, if you feed us, we will come. We jumped into his Rolls-Royce Silver Cloud and drove over to Universal City to a popular watering hole and Chinese restaurant. We both agreed it was too early to eat, so we went straight to the bar. By now we were calling each other Jim and Dick instead of James and Richard, and Dick was glad-handing several regulars connected to the film industry.

An attractive couple called us over and Dick introduced me to Hoyt Bowers and his lovely wife, who happened to be from Fort Worth. When I told her I was from Dallas, we had an immediate connection, which, of course, called for more drinks. I was starting to feel the

F Troop cast without me. *Author Collection.*

effects of several vodka tonics, but Dick showed no signs of inebriation at all. I was impressed.

It turned out that Hoyt Bowers was the casting director at Warner Brothers Studio. He told me that they were assembling a cast for a pilot and he thought I might be perfect for one of the roles. He suggested I have my agent call his office the following Monday.

A couple of drinks later, Dick and I decided we weren't hungry yet, and he suggested another watering hole in Hollywood. Fortunately, we couldn't find the Silver Cloud. After a half hour of looking, we had sobered up enough to give up and call a cab. I took the cab, and Dick called a friend who spotted the Rolls not fifty feet from the restaurant entrance. I paid off the cabbie, as it was time to celebrate finding the Rolls. I woke the next day on top of my bed, but I have no memory of how I got there. I also forgot about Mr. and Mrs. Bowers, Warner Brothers, the Kohner Agency, the pilot, and any other details.

The following Monday afternoon I got a call from Walter Kohner, who was very agitated.

"James! Do you know where you are supposed to be right now?"

"Uh . . . not really, sir."

"Get over to Warner Brothers as fast as you can. You are reading for a pilot! They are waiting for you in Hoyt Bowers's office!"

I was staying in Don Henley's apartment about fifteen minutes away from Burbank. I changed my shirt, splashed on some Old Spice, ran down the stairs, and jumped into Shirley Boone's VW Bug that she had so graciously lent me. In those days, the freeways were wide open, and I floored it down Sunset Boulevard, turned left on the 101 through the Cahuenga Pass, and flew down the hill to Burbank.

I was praying as hard as I could trying to cut a deal with God where I would never have another drink of alcohol if he would just make the people at Warner Brothers stay put until I got there. At that moment, I saw the big water tower that displayed the WB insignia. A friendly guard at the gate let me through and told me where to go. I raced up the stairs to an empty anteroom. It appeared as though I would be the last batter up. I have since learned that the last actor in often has an advantage, but I didn't know that then. I hurriedly wrote my name on the casting sheet and noticed there had been about twenty guys ahead of me. The secretary handed me a script and showed me the scene I was reading for. She told me to tap on her frosted sliding-glass window when I was ready. I thanked her and told her I would. I took a deep breath and glanced at the title: *F Troop.*

I couldn't believe my eyes! F Troop Sixth Armored Cavalry was the outfit I was assigned to for basic and advanced infantry training in Fort Knox, Kentucky. I thought, *Lord, you have really done something this time.*

I studied the pages I was there to read for, and a few minutes later I tapped on her window. She smiled and said, "That was quick," and ushered me into a large office. Hoyt Bowers wasn't the only one present. There was William T. Orr, head of Warner Brothers Television; Richard Bluel, vice president in charge of television production; Ed James and Seaman Jacobs, who wrote the script; Hy Averback, the executive producer; and Charles Rondeau, the director.

Mr. Rondeau shook my hand and told me Mr. Bowers would read with me. I nonchalantly tossed my script over on Mr. Rondeau's desk. I was always a quick study, and I wanted to look them in the eye instead of reading with my head down.

"Ready when you are, Sir."

To my surprise, all those men who could change my life exploded with laughter. I looked at them as if I had done something wrong. After all, I thought the scene hadn't started yet. I was wrong, of course. The scene had begun when I walked into that room. They saw the character through me, and it did not escape their attention that I had a little Texas twang. The accent that I tried so hard to eliminate in New York had once again been an asset in Hollywood.

We began the scene and immediately there was more laughter. The writers were taking notes. I began to relax a little. The scene was about meeting our new captain and I was to be his orderly as well as the troop bugler. When Dobbs saw how inept the new captain was, he began to relax. It was exactly what was happening right there in Mr. Bowers's big office. We finished the scene and Mr. Rondeau shook my hand and told me they would let me know. I thanked them and left. I thanked the secretary on my way out as well, and the two of us crossed our fingers as I returned the script. I started down the stairs thinking I had done pretty well, but the odds of doing a pilot were huge.

I had taken only three or four steps when Charlie Rondeau burst out of the office. He shouted, "Hampton, come back here!"

I thought I had done something wrong. As I raced up the stairs, he broke into a wide smile.

"You're our bugler."

F Troop with Larry Storch. *Author Collection.*

He reached over to the young lady who handed him the script and offered it to me.

"Here. You are going to need this."

Kenny, Larry, and me in the '90s. *Author Collection.*

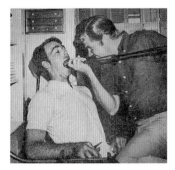

Practicing dentistry on Ken Berry. *Author Collection.*

Ken Berry was the best physical comedian I never saw. No doubt this was due to his background as a dancer. He made those pratfalls look so easy. Kenny taught me a few tricks, but the only one I was ever good at was the "trip." After *F Troop* ended, Kenny went on to appear on almost every show on television and had the good fortune to star in two hugely popular, long-running sitcoms, *Mayberry R. F. D.* and *Mama's Family.* Before *F Troop,* we had actually worked together on an episode of *Dr. Kildare* (who didn't work on *Dr. Kildare*?). Kenny, Bob Denver, and I played three young doctors. One day, when we were on our lunch break, Bob mentioned that he was auditioning the next week for some "crazy show" about some castaways on an island. I guess he booked it! Professionally, Kenny and I crossed paths many times after *F Troop* ended on both television shows and in movies like *Love American Style, The Cat From Outer Space,* and *Mama's Family.* Personally, we remained friends until he passed away. He was one swell guy.

People always ask me what it was like to work on *F Troop.* First of all, it wasn't "work" at all. It was like going to a party every week. Back then, I couldn't wait for Mondays. Larry Storch was just one reason why.

To this day, I cannot look, listen or even think about Larry Storch without laughing. In my book, he is the Grand Poobah of Comedy and a sweeter man you'll never meet. His pet name for me on set was "Jim-Jim," and it's what he still calls me.

Early in the first season of *F Troop,* Larry, who became my lifelong friend, was challenged with riding a horse for an upcoming scene. Hampton to the rescue. As a Texan, I saw it as my duty to give Larry his first riding lesson. I

With Vicki Lawrence in *Mama's Family. Author Collection.*

suggested that during a break in filming, we procure two of the more good-natured steeds and take a little ride on the back lot at Warner Brothers. With assurance that I wouldn't leave him stranded, Larry was cautiously optimistic. Off

Taking direction from director Charles Rondeau. *Author Collection.*

we rode. I was in the middle of giving Larry some important pointers about "leading" the horse with the reins when it dawned on me that I had left my wallet on my set chair. It contained a whole twelve dollars. Vowing to promptly return, I galloped away leaving a distraught-looking Larry atop his horse under a shade tree. Once back on the lot, I became distracted and ended up sharing lunch and bad jokes with one of the stunt guys from the show. Suddenly, I remembered leaving Larry. I took off as quickly as I could but did not find him where I had left him. Panicked, I began roaming the back-lot range. "Perhaps he rode back," I thought. A preposterous idea.

When I finally found him, there was Larry, head hanging down, still on the horse but in the middle of a field where the horse, reins loose, was happily eating sweet grass. Fortunately, my pal was very forgiving and relieved to see me. Confused, I asked him how he had ended up in the field so far from where I left him. He answered "Oh

Jim Jim, everything was going just swell until I dropped the handle bars!"

Larry and Tuck had that magic chemistry that all the great comedy duos—Laurel and Hardy, Abbott and Costello, Martin and Lewis—had. It was pure entertainment to watch them interact with one another off screen as well. Once, I was sitting in my set chair going over my script when I saw Larry pacing back and forth by the craft service table. He was clearly worried about something. Tuck walked up and, observing the same thing I had, asked him what was wrong. Larry replied that he had lost the expensive new pair of glasses that his wife, Norma, had bought for him and that, when she found out, she was going to be very upset. Tuck read off a list of places where Larry might have left his specs, but Larry shook his head and told him that he had already looked in all of those locations.

"Well," asked Tuck, "Have you checked the pocket of your set chair?"

F Troop cast in the Rose Parade, 1967. *Author Collection.*

With Joe Brooks and the littlest trooper. *Author Collection.*

Agarn and Dobbs together again. *Author Collection.*

"Oh no!" said Larry, "I can't do that."

"Why not?" asked Tuck.

To which Larry replied "Because if they ain't there, then they're really lost!"

My bride, Mary, who is half Korean, adores Larry and he loves her to pieces. They greet each other the same way each time they meet. Larry throws open his arms and says to her "Mary! Darling! You look like a million Yen!" Mary goes in for the hug and replies "Thank you honey, but that's only about twenty-six cents." She's going to leave me for him one day. I just know it.

Just a few weeks after *F Troop* first aired, I received a call from a woman who claimed to be with the musician's union. Having known many musicians from my days at North Texas State College, I assumed it was a prank and said as much. The woman caller had no sense of humor. "No," she argued. "You're playing a musical instrument and you are putting a musician out of work. You must join the union." I hesitated and then said "Look, lady, you watch the show next Tuesday night and if what you think I'm playing is music, I'll join."

I never heard from her again.

FIFTEEN
FAME

Burt Reynolds once told me, "Fame is going to bed Wednesday night and nobody knows who you are and waking up Thursday morning and everyone knows who you are."

In my case, I seem to be stuck at the Wednesday night part.

It happened again yesterday on the way home from a celebrity golf tournament. I stopped for gas, and when I went inside to get my card swiped, one of the ladies behind the counter asked the dreaded question, "Are you somebody famous?" There is no way to answer this question. There never has been, and there never will be. If I say, "Why yes ma'am, I guess you could put it that way. I have been an actor for a long time," then she will demand proof. "Oh yeah, what am I supposed to know you from?"

Now I'm really screwed, because if she doesn't know where she's seen me, how am I going to know? Fortunately, over the years I have gotten pretty good at approximating the age of the person I am talking to, and I can usually come up with the right answer. Or at least one that will satisfy them so I can get going. I have an age gauge that I go by:

Twenty to thirty years = *Sling Blade*
Thirty to forty years = *Teen Wolf, China Syndrome*
Forty to fifty years (Female) = *The Tonight Show*
Forty to fifty years (Male) = *The Longest Yard, The Rockford Files*
Fifty to sixty years (Female) = *The Doris Day Show, Love American Style*
Fifty to sixty years (Male) = *F Troop, The Longest Yard*
Sixty years to "The Old Pine Box" = *F Troop, Gunsmoke, Gomer Pyle*

Best picture of me EVER! *Author Collection.*

Honored to receive this plaque on the Walk of Fame in Kanab, Utah. *Author Collection.*

I pegged the gals in the Chevron station to be around forty to fifty, but I struck out. I tried everything, but no soap. Finally, one of the nice ladies remembered.

"I know what it was! It was that one with Burt Reynolds."

"*The Longest Yard?*"

"No."

Hanging out on the set of *Iron Cowboy* with Burt Reynolds. *Author Collection.*

I had fun on *Love, American Style*. *Author Collection.*

Oh boy! Phyllis Davis and me on *Love, American Style*. *Author Collection.*

"*W. W. and the Dixie Dancekings?*"

"No."

"*The Man Who Loved Cat Dancing?*"

"No."

"*Hustle? The Iron Cowboy?*"

I was starting to get frantic.

"No. That other one. You know where you're rafting down the river.

"*Deliverance?*"

"Yeah!" They both began nodding vigorously. "You were real good in that."

Silence. Then I said:

"Thank you, Ma'am."

That happens a lot. I have learned through experience that once a person has decided they have identified you there is no use arguing that they are thinking of Ned Beatty or anyone else for that matter. On one occasion, at another celebrity golf tournament, Ned and I exchanged name tags for the entire evening. When he was introduced, I stood up and when I was introduced he stood up. No one seemed to notice. Of course, I got the best of the deal. I wonder if he has to explain *Hawmps!* to people.

Some entertainers are famous for doing it all. Veteran stars like Debbie Reynolds, Gene Kelly, Judy Garland, and Donald O'Connor could act, sing and dance. Today, we've got Christopher Walken, Meryl Streep and . . . disagree if you must, but . . . J. Lo. I had the pleasure of working with someone who was a "triple threat" as well. The comedienne, journalist, and television producer

70

(Top Left) Miriam Flynn and me in *Maggie*, 1981. (Top Right) From the set of *Maggie*. (Bottom) Cast and crew of Erma Bombeck's show *Maggie*. *Courtesy of Matthew Bombeck and The Estate of Erma Bombeck.*

Erma Bombeck. She had a sweet little sitcom in the 1980s called Maggie and I played the husband of the star, Miriam Flynn. It followed the life of a working mom and her family and, I believe, was loosely based on Erma's similar experiences. She was as funny and kind as she was talented. They say fame is fleeting. Well, I'm still laughing at Erma's jokes, singing along with Debbie, and trying to shuffle my feet like Gene. So, I beg to differ.

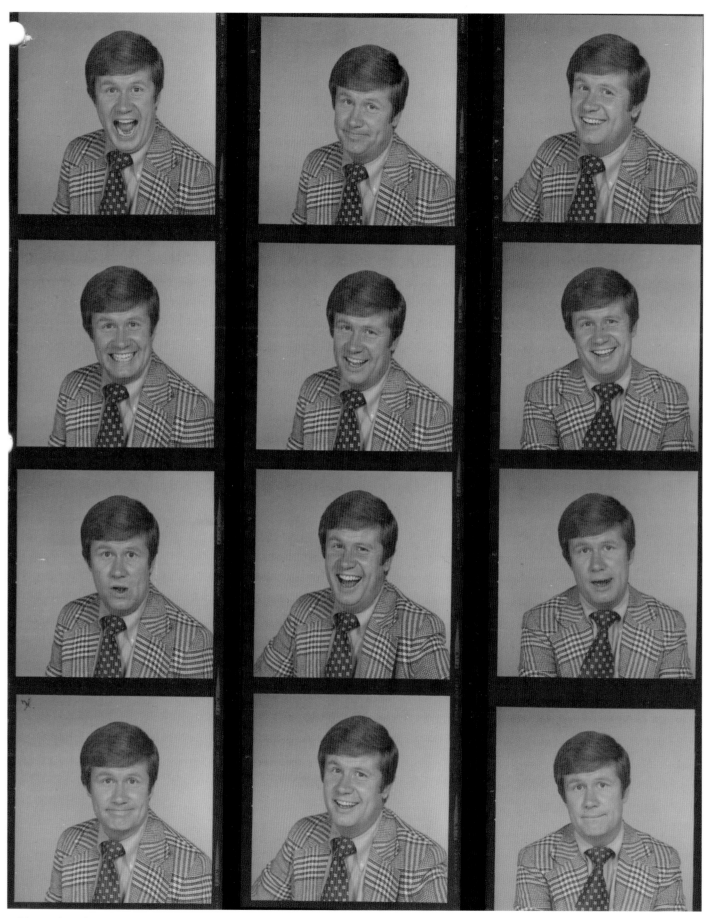

Publicity shots for *The Jim Hampton Show*. *Author Collection*.

I had a shot at being a talk-show host. I did a pilot for CBS called—and this took a lot of research and planning—*The Jim Hampton Show*. It was a wonderful experience. Rick Hurst was my Ed McMahon, and Larry Cansler, a good friend from North Texas, was my Doc Severinsen. My guests included the lovely and funny Elaine Joyce, Lee J. Cobb, and of course, Burt Reynolds.

It turned out that lots of things were going on that day. First of all, Dinah Shore's show had been cancelled. CBS had a slot for her. Hours before the *The Jim Hampton Show*, written by yours truly, had its debut in front of an enthusiastic audience, the rug had been pulled out from under our feet. A deal between CBS and Dinah's representatives had been cut to fill CBS's daytime programming hole. That would be the hole that I had been anxious to fill. Always the trailblazer, I was, to my knowledge, the

first show to be cancelled before the pilot was taped.

Burt gave me the details in my dressing room (soon to be Dinah's, I reckoned), and we decided not to tell anyone else, not even my producer.

We went on and gave them all we had. Elaine was perky and delightful, Lee was droll, Burt charmed the ladies, and we had a great ending. Our last guest (and I do mean last) was a woman psychologist who taught us how to get rid of aggression and pent-up anger by passing out *batacas*, which resembled padded cricket bats. As our theme music began under Larry's baton, we were whacking the crap out of each other. The audience went nuts. We were a hit! You could feel the love. We were Oprah!

CBS showed the pilot on December 25 at five in the afternoon. My own mother didn't even watch it.

The Dinah Shore Show hired me to write jokes for her.

SIXTEEN
HUMILITY

Humility is a wonderful thing, they tell me. It certainly seems to be an admirable trait when you see it in others. However, actors sometimes have a little trouble in this area. Sometimes an actor has a streak of good luck and lands some good parts. You make a movie that everyone is talking about and all of a sudden, you're a celebrity. People start treating you with a certain amount of deference. You get good tables in restaurants. You feel like you have arrived and actually deserve this new level of respect. That's when the good Lord steps in and smacks you on the back of the hand with a ruler. It stings for a little bit, but that is the sort of thing that builds character and reminds you of what is truly important.

I had had had some successes in Hollywood, not the least of which was being a regular on *F Troop*. The show had caught on with the public, and the cast was being invited to a number of publicity outings. Naturally, the invitations were initially aimed at the show's stars—Larry Storch, Forrest Tucker, and Ken Berry—but, finally, I received an invitation to go to my first premiere.

The movie was a big-budget epic called *The Battle of the Bulge*. It was being shown at the Egyptian Theater on Hollywood Boulevard. I was very excited. The dress was formal—tuxedos and evening gowns.

Actually, I was just dying for an excuse to wear a tuxedo that my pal Pat Boone had given me. I'll do my best to describe it. The jacket was a startling blue velvet job with extra-wide plaid lapels and velvet buttons in abundance. The pants were the same blue-and-burgundy plaid as the lapels. These were the days of bellbottoms, so the bells had matching blue velvet inserts and lots more buttons. The shirt was something Cornel Wilde could have worn in a sword fight with Oscar Wilde. Liberace wore more conservative shirts. The bowtie was the same blue velvet and about four inches wide. I wore patent leather zip-up boots with heels that made me taller, and I thought I looked grand. The big night arrived.

I had recently purchased my first new car. The Borgward Isabella with an electric transmission that I had purchased in New York for five hundred dollars had finally given up the ghost. I traded it in to Ralph Williams Ford for a powder-blue Ford Fairlane 500. After all, I was making five hundred dollars a week on *F Troop*. I felt I deserved a handsome automobile. Besides, it sort of matched Pat's velvet jacket.

I left Encino on the 101, purred past the Hollywood Bowl, and took the exit for Hollywood Boulevard. Following the traffic, I filtered into the slow-moving lineup for the premiere. I could see the big searchlights scanning the skies from blocks away. Cheering fans were packed into bleachers outside the Egyptian. Uniformed valets were taking the cars as the stars emerged and were welcomed on the red carpet by Army Archerd. Then I noticed something. In this whole line of cars, mine was the only American-made, powder-blue Ford Fairlane 500. There were several Rolls, a few Bentleys, and some limos, but nothing in powder blue. They were all black and very expensive looking. Suddenly, I didn't feel so flush. The thought came to me to peel out of the line and head back to the Valley.

As I neared the drop-off area, I noticed that a fan from the bleachers was acting as a scout. He would run up to a car, peer inside to identify the celebrity, then triumphantly announce who it was to the cheering throng. This was his gig: run up to the car, look inside, turn around, and announce "Mike Connors!" or "Sandra Dee!" When I got near enough, he came tearing up to the Ford, stuck his head in, looked at me, turned around, and made his announcement.

"Nobody!"

And off he ran to the next big, black shiny car behind me. It took a little bloom off the rose, I can tell you.

As if I hadn't learned my lesson yet, here's another humble pie that smacked me square in the puss when I wasn't looking.

A few friends were coming over so I ran to the market to get a few items. Sometimes, when I'm in a hurry, I leave my shopping cart at the top of an aisle while I run down to get what I need. This was what I was doing on this particular Sunday afternoon. Push the cart, leave it at the top of an aisle, race down for an item, race back to the cart, deposit the item in the cart, and repeat the process in another aisle.

I stopped to catch my breath and go over what I needed next. Out of the corner of my eye I saw a couple of nice little old ladies who were smiling, whispering, and pointing in my direction. *Drat!* I thought. I had been recognized. I had seen this sort of behavior before when someone had spotted me, but I was in a hurry. I didn't have time while they dug around in their purses for scraps of paper and a pen so I could sign my name for their grandchildren. *Sorry girls*, I thought, *but I'm a man on a mission.*

So, I raced away with the cart, parked it, retrieved some onion dip, and trotted back to the cart. The ladies were standing by the frozen canapés. They looked entirely bemused. They were probably nice old dames who remembered me from *The Doris Day Show*. If I weren't in such a hurry . . . and then I thought, *Hold your horses there, pal. Are you so busy that you can't be kind to a couple of fans? Have you become such a big shot you have forgotten your roots?* I was ashamed.

Well, they weren't going away. *I may as well get it over with* I thought. So, I decided to pause by the potato chips and give them a little time to gather the courage to approach a handsome television and movie star like me. Sure enough, here they came. I thought I'd help them out a little. I figured they probably knew me but wouldn't remember from what show. However, I was laying odds it was as Leroy B. Simpson on *The Doris Day Show.*

Instead, here's what happened.

"Excuse me young man."

I acted surprised, but friendly and approachable. "Yes, Ma'am?"

"You're pushing our cart!"

I actually enjoy being recognized, especially since I have retired and moved back to Texas. I have a little fun with people. It often goes like this:

"Excuse me, but you know who you look like?"

"No, who?"

"That guy."

"What guy?"

"You know. That actor guy."

"What actor guy?"

"You know that guy in (fill in the blank)."

"Oh yeah? I've been told that before."

"You even sound like him!"

"Well, there's a good reason for that."

"What?"

"I'm him."

"No!"

"Yeah."

"No!"

"Honest. Here's my driver's license, see? That's me!"

"Well I'll be danged. What are you doing here?"

"I live here."

"How come?"

"I like it here. Don't you like it here?"

"Oh yeah, but I ain't in the movies."

I don't think that most people are rude by nature, they are just skeptical.

"I know you from somewhere. Do you go to my church?"

"No, ma'am. I'm an actor."

"No, that's not it. Did you used to work at Blah Blah Blah, Inc.?"

"No, ma'am. I'm an actor."

"Hmmm. Maybe we went to school together."

"Yeah. That must be it."

"I knew it. I never forget a face!"

Sometimes the limits are stretched. I was in the Topanga Plaza Mall in California one beautiful summer day, minding my own business and doing a little shopping, when I noticed two women giving me the once-over. One of them had a T-shirt on that announced "I'm a Virgin" on the front and, "It's an old T-shirt" on the back. The one with the T-shirt was looking at me in annoyance, as though I was upsetting her in some way. They began walking my way.

When I was a bartender in New York, I had seen people just like her coming into the restaurant looking for trouble. I was always right. I was right this time. But I am a very non-confrontational sort of guy, and I have always believed it is better to avoid trouble than to be sucked into unpleasant situations. I turned away and had taken a few steps when the T-shirt grabbed me by the arm and spun me around. She was looking at me like I was an ex-husband who owed her money.

"Where am I supposed to know you from?"

A loaded question if ever I heard one. I knew where this was headed. No matter how hard I tried, no matter how many shows I would name, she would not be satisfied. But I would give it my best shot anyway. I put on my "Aw shucks" smile and said, almost apologetically, "I'm an actor."

Her girlfriend giggled as only a forty-five-year-old, three-pack-a-day, multiple-divorcee can giggle. It ended with a lot of coughing and wheezing.

"Oh yeah?" said the T-shirt. "Name something you've been in."

I wasn't going down that road. I had been there before. Then it came to me. I stepped a little closer. This time my smile was genuine.

"I'll tell you what. You name all the movies you've seen, and if I have been in any of them, I'll tell you."

There was a moment of stunned silence before they slunk away. Wait, was that the *1812 Overture* I was hearing through the mall's speaker system?

RANDOM OCCURRENCES

With acting, as far as the job goes, it is all or nothing. Either you get the part or you don't. I've often thought that there ought to be at least a prize for coming in second, but it doesn't work that way. If there had been a trophy, ribbon, or certificate for every time I got the short end of the stick, my den walls would be quite impressive. The reasons for not getting the role are often quite imaginative. In any case, here are a few quickies about the part that got away.

MISTAKEN IDENTITY

When I first got to Hollywood, for some reason I booked just about every role I was up for. Sometimes I didn't even have to read for the part. My agent would be called, a script would be delivered to my home, and terms would be agreed upon. Then things inexplicably changed. Suddenly there didn't seem to be any market for Jim Hampton. At one point, I stopped into my agent's office and asked if there was any interest for me on the horizon. I was told that just that morning there was a request for a "Jim Hampton type." When my agent informed the caller that the agency handled Jim Hampton, the reply was . . . "No." It was very puzzling. Why had I suddenly become a pariah?

If it wasn't for the determination of a director that I worked with many times on *The Doris Day Show*, it would still be a mystery.

The director had been signed to direct several episodes of *Bracken's World*. His first show had a part in it that was tailor-made for me. When he recommended me for the role, the executive producer told him I was unsuitable. When pressed for an answer, the producer maintained he had heard I was difficult to work with. "Difficult" meant a person who caused needless delays that cost money. "Difficult" as in Marilyn Monroe, James Dean, or Marlon Brando. At least I was in good company. My director friend hit the ceiling.

"What are you talking about? I've worked with Jimmy many times and never had a problem."

The producer shrugged his shoulders.

"All I know is he has a reputation for being a problem on the set, a real prima donna. We're on too tight a schedule to put up with that type of crap."

"This is the craziest thing I've ever heard. Look, don't cast the role yet. Give me a day to get to the bottom of this thing."

He made several calls to casting agents who had never used me, and they all said the same thing: I was a real pain in the ass. Finally, one of the casting people told my director friend a story he had heard about me causing shooting delays, complaining about the scripts, acting unprofessionally, and so forth except he used a different first name for me. Let's say it was Don.

"Who the hell is Don Hampton?" my friend wanted to know.

"That's the guy you were asking me about, isn't it?"

"No, I was asking about Jim Hampton."

"Oh . . . yeah. Sorry."

I got the part on *Bracken's World* and my career returned to normal, as if there is such a thing.

THE PUBLICITY GIRL

After completing *Hawmps!,* the movie about camels in the US Cavalry, there came the time for publicity. Christopher Connelly and I were designated certain cities to cover, and Frank Inn, the animal trainer, along with Valentine the Camel, would meet us in the larger cities. It was a grueling pace of twenty-seven cities in twenty-one days, crisscrossing the country several times, and seldom getting a good night's sleep.

In each city we were met by a publicity person who would make sure that Joe Camp's money was being spent wisely and every waking minute was scheduled for talk shows, press luncheons, and photo opportunities. It was always nice to meet up with Chris and swap stories about our adventures. By the time we met up in Boston, we were both goofy from fatigue and the endless questions about camels.

We were met at the airport by the publicity girl who was taking us to dinner. We ate at Bookbinders, where the food was excellent, but the publicity girl talked nonstop. She gave us our schedules, which included a press breakfast at 8:00 a.m., a local TV show at 9:30 a.m., photos with a camel at the zoo, and on and on. The publicity girl was extremely thorough and very enthusiastic. Absolutely the last type of person you want around when you are about to pass out from exhaustion. Chris actually nodded off once over dinner.

We took a cab back to our hotel around 11:00 p.m., and the publicity girl was still yapping away about how important it was for us to be on time and chipper the next day. Chris and I had rooms across the hall from each other, as she had seen to that earlier when

Going on a camel ride on *Hawmps!* with Chris Connelly and Jack Elam. *Courtesy of Joe Camp.*

she checked us in. She finally gave us our keys and we opened our doors hoping she would get the hint that we were ready to call it a night, when she launched into a long story about other celebrities and actors she had come into contact with.

About that time, two couples on their way to the elevator were approaching us. I looked at Chris and gave him a wink that said, *Follow my lead.*

The two couples were less than five yards away when, in a loud and irritated voice, I exclaimed, "Fifty dollars? That's ridiculous!"

Four stunned faces stared briefly at the tableau as Chris and I entered our rooms and locked the doors. The publicity girl was a little quieter after that.

PALM SPRINGS

Pat Boone is responsible for my love affair with golf. He used to host a wonderful few days of golf in the Pacific Northwest at an area called Ocean Shores, Washington. The first year we were invited I borrowed some clubs from Don Henley (which were originally Pat's) and off we went. I was hooked from the very start. Meeting all the wonderful celebrities that came every year, eating freshly caught Columbia River salmon cooked by Native Americans, and the tournament itself, were things I came to look forward to all year. I had done a couple of years on *F Troop* by then and was starting to realize that I might be a celebrity as well. So, when an invitation came from

Milton Berle and my buddy Willie Shoemaker to play in their golf tournament in Palm Springs, I felt I had arrived, and I eagerly accepted.

The information in the invitation packet included a request for an auction item. Although I was doing *The Doris Day Show* by then, the only thing I could think of to bring was the bugle I used on *F Troop*. I packed up Don's clubs (I never actually returned them, as he had taken up tennis by then) and pointed my trusty Ford Fairlane 500 toward the desert.

When I arrived at the lodge in Bermuda Dunes, my room was full of goodies. A beautiful professional tour bag

My favorite pastime. *Author Collection.*

with my name on it was the first thing I noticed; there were also balls, golf shoes, golf shirts, liquor, a basket of fruit, and a welcome letter signed by Willie and Uncle Milty. This celebrity thing was starting to work out!

There was a program with all the celebrities' pictures in alphabetical order and their tee times for the following day. There I was, right between George Gobel and Dennis James. They even had a blank page that simply said "Autographs."

A banquet was being held that evening, and it was requested that those who had brought auction items come slightly early so that their item could be cataloged and displayed. I had just enough time to shower, slap on some Hai Karate cologne, and dress for the occasion. I laid out my polyester plaid sport coat with wide lapels, my powder-blue polyester-knit bell-bottom pants with a two-inch-wide white belt, and my white patent leather zip-up-the-side boots. I won't even try to describe the shirt and tie.

I got there early, smelling good, and was profusely thanked by a volunteer for the thoughtful donation of a "trumpet." I assured her it was nothing at all and left her looking curiously at my bugle.

I found my assigned table and waited for the festivities. After a short time, people began to filter in. Soon a couple was headed my way, a portly gentleman with a large pinky ring and his tiny wife who was wearing the rest of the jewelry store. What really caught my attention was the almost floor-length chinchilla coat she was wearing. It was 108 degrees outside, but I guess she must have had problems with drafts and wasn't taking any chances. Her husband, however, appeared to be suffering from the heat and was wearing sunglasses indoors. He began drumming his fingers on the table and looking at a small card that had my name on it. He appeared to be irritated about something.

Although I seemed to be entirely invisible to both of them, I was about to introduce myself when the gentleman spoke in a loud voice.

"James Hampton? Who the hell is James Hampton?"

His wife didn't seem to know or care and devoted most of her time to the primping of her hair and the chewing of her gum. She was busy but she worked in a shrug.

I thought maybe I had better go back to my room and come back later. After a few drinks perhaps this guy will be in a better mood. *Oh crap!* He was looking my way.

"You pay $1,500 to play in one of these things and what do you get? Sinatra? Hope? Nah! We got a James Hampton! You ever hear of a James Hampton?"

Without thinking a nanosecond, I shook my head and shrugged sympathetically.

I know, I know, but it seemed like a good idea at the time. I thought it was brilliant, as a matter of fact. What could a little white lie like that hurt? After all, I didn't want to embarrass the guy in front of his wife . . . or hooker. Yep, I did the right thing. The waiter came over. I felt a little dry.

"What are you drinking?" Pinky Ring shouts.

"Vodka tonic," I answer.

"Bring us three vodka tonics and keep 'em coming," and he hands the waiter a twenty.

Other people begin to arrive. Each one is grilled by Pinky. Nobody had ever heard of James Hampton. This was a little more complicated than I had originally thought.

Some of these people seem perfectly nice, and I was lying to them. Still, we were all bonding in our mutual disgust for that Hampton guy. Not only that, the bastard hadn't even had the courtesy to show up! We kept looking around the room to see if we could spot somebody that might be him. With each cocktail we grew more pissed off at this stuck-up actor and more convivial with each other. The empty chair next to me was proof enough that Hampton was a no-show.

McLean Stevenson was the emcee, and his opening remarks were riotously funny. I had known him since we were in New York when I was a struggling actor/bartender and he was in advertising. Mac began by auctioning off two muskets from the Revolutionary War that had been in his family for over a hundred years. They went for $2,500 each. Then, he decided to auction off the bugle. I was mortified. Two Revolutionary War muskets that went for five grand and now is the time to auction off a prop from a TV show that lasted only two years? But then Mac had an idea.

"This next item is just great. It's the actual bugle that my friend Jimmy Hampton blew on the hit show *F Troop*! How about a nice hand for James Hampton? Come on up here Jim and auction this thing off. Where are you, Jim?"

I wanted the earth to swallow me up. Then I heard Big Guy say, "Yeah, where is the bastard?"

Everybody at our table was craning our necks to see where this cur was. I was looking hard, too, while staying behind a column out of Mac's sight line.

"Well I guess Jim had to go to the bathroom. So, what am I offered for the bugle?"

It went for three hundred bucks. I excused myself from my newfound friends and unsteadily slunk away.

I must admit that even all these years later, when I think of the expression on Pinky Ring's face when, back in his room, he took a look at the celebrity pages in the program and he saw my smiling mug between George and Dennis . . . it made it all worthwhile.

Still tootin' my bugle. *Author Collection.*

EIGHTEEN
THE STARS

BURT REYNOLDS

I met Burt when he was part of the wonderful cast of *Gunsmoke*. He played Quint, the half-breed Indian blacksmith. He did something very kind that day, and I will never forget it.

It was the first day of shooting, on my very first television show, which just happened to be the number one show in the country. I had gone to Los Angeles to be a part of the Academy Awards celebration in 1963. Molly Scott, a girl in my acting class, and I were in a nominated film in the Live Action Short Subject category. It was shot in a garage in upstate New York. Kind of sounds like a porno film, but it wasn't. It was a sweet boy-meets-girl flick that was produced and directed by a bartender in Greenwich Village, who also happened to have the hots for Molly.

We didn't win, but my new agent Paul Kohner had submitted me for a wonderful role on *Gunsmoke* while I was in town. Against all odds and the misgivings of the director, Harry Harris, I was chosen for the part. There was a lot riding on me being able to deliver. Not to mention they were paying me all the money in the world . . . $750.00, which was about five times what I was making a week at The Orchidia restaurant, including tips.

The entire veteran cast and crew couldn't have been more friendly or helpful. Amanda Blake/Miss Kitty, Milburn "Millie" Stone/Doc, Glenn Strange/bartender (and a great Frankenstein monster at Universal), Dennis Weaver/Chester, and speaking of monsters, James Arness, who was the alien in *The Thing*, were all delightful.

Burt's stardom was just beginning with two hit series under his belt, including the helmsman on the television series *Riverboat*. The veteran crew was the best at what they did. Everyone was relaxed as we sat in our canvas set chairs and told jokes. Well, they told jokes. I was too scared. I was sure this couldn't be real. Sooner or later two guys in overcoats and fedoras were going to show up and

With Burt Reynolds on the *Evening Shade* set. *Author Collection.*

motion me to come with them. I would be busted for pretending to be an actor.

One of them would say, "You da guy dats havin' his cake and eatin' it too? Come wid us, smart guy."

We had shot a simple two-character scene with Burt and me, and the next set-up was "coverage." After the "master," or "two-shot" in this case, we would shoot "singles" and close-ups. Burt knew I was nervous, and he slapped me on the back and said, "What are you worried about? You're doing fine."

The assistant director told us the camera was ready and showed me my mark, which was a little wooden capital "T" showing me where I needed to stand. The photographer pointed to my "key light." It was a whole new vocabulary, and I hadn't a clue what they were telling me much of the time.

Harry Harris came over and said, "Just do what you did in the master. That was fine. Do you want a rehearsal or do you want to go for one?"

I nodded dumbly. "Let's go for it."

The assistant director shouted, "All right people. Settle down! We are going for one. Places, please. Quiet on the set!"

As he walked by me, he muttered, "You're doing fine."

The makeup man said I was getting a little shiny and, as he patted me down, he said, "You're gonna be fine."

A little shiny? I thought. *I'm sweating buckets here! Now where is Burt?*

A long, ear-splitting bell began to ring. Work lights were turned off. It was a night scene. We were on a soundstage on the Dodge City main street. It was all there, just like we saw it on TV; dirt streets, wooden sidewalks, the Long Branch Saloon, wagons, and horses.

The assistant director yelled, "Background . . . action!" and the atmosphere actors dressed as townsfolk and cowboys began gliding by soundlessly.

"Speed!" was shouted by someone in the sound department.

A fellow walked up with a clapper and said something I didn't understand and then banged the clapper about an inch from the tip of my nose.

Harry's voice said, "And . . . Action."

So, I started acting. I heard Burt giving his lines and spotted him next to the camera. In the script, and in the master we had shot, after a few lines, my Jeb character interrupted his Quint character. When that cue came, I was on it, exactly as I had been taught in the theater, and exactly as I had done in the master which everyone seemed to like. We played the scene out and the director said, "Cut." I thought, *That was perfect!* Then I saw Harry turn to the sound man who sat a few yards away from the camera. He was at a soundboard with earphones on twiddling a myriad of dials and buttons.

Harry asked the sound man, "Sound?"

The guy shook his head and said, "No good, Mr. Harris . . . overlap."

Harry looked at me suspiciously and said. "Once again, please."

The assistant director shouted, "First positions!"

It was like when you see a movie played backwards. Everyone, everything, every person, wagon, horse and mule, goes back to square one. Bells ring, adjustments are made, lights are lit and unlit, and the powder puffs come out.

Harry strolled over and quietly said, "Watch the overlap."

I nodded as if I understood. I didn't, of course. In my vast experience before the camera—one twenty-minute short subject—I had never heard the word overlap or why I needed to watch it. My mind began to race trying to find a clue.

I knew that this overlap business had something to do with sound. Should I speak louder or softer? Bells rang and clappers clapped and I made a hasty decision. I wasn't interrupting Burt fast enough. I needed to get there a little faster somehow. I was glad I figured that one out. I would show them a dizzyingly quick interruption! Burt was by the camera again. This time he gave a friendly wave, even pointed at himself as though he was saying, "Here I am."

Harry called "Action."

We began to run the scene again, but this time I was ready. When we came to that place again, I pounced like a rabid mongoose. I knew I had absolutely nailed it. Harry must have got what he wanted because he said, "cut" right away. I was exhilarated! It was short lived.

Harry turned to the sound man who said, "NG, Harry."

NG? No good? I was dumbfounded.

Then I heard the assistant director shout, "Once more from the top! Let's get going people!"

He was looking nervously at his watch. The background folks scurried back to their positions, a few cast glances in my direction, some nervous, some sympathetic. Even the horses were starting to look at me a little funny. Harry walked over. *Well,* I thought, *at least I'll get some direction.* I did.

Harry said, "Watch the overlap," and returned to his chair by the camera. The hair on the back of my head was wet and perspiration seemed to be running into my boots.

I didn't see how I could get my cue in any faster, but I would try. Bells rang and buzzers buzzed. The wardrobe guy whispered to me not to raise my arms as my shirt was wet in the arm pits. Then Burt did the most peculiar thing. Just before action he waved at me and went into an over-the-top pantomime.

He pointed to his wrist and exaggeratedly mouthed, "Watch!" Then he pointed to his chest and mouthed, "Me!"

I couldn't believe it. At this critical moment he wanted to know what time it was?

Harry called, "Action."

Once again, I began acting as Burt continued gesturing and mouthing, "Watch me, watch me!" twice more. When

Burt Reynolds's "Best Little Chicken Breasts in Texas" (It'll Put Hair On Your Chest!)

INGREDIENTS

6 to 10 chicken breast halves, skinned and boned
½ cup vegetable oil
1 cup lime or lemon juice
3 teaspoons garlic powder
2 tablespoons minced jalapeño pepper
½ teaspoon salt
¼ teaspoon pepper
Lime wedges, jalapeño peppers, cherry tomatoes,
    and parsley for garnish

DIRECTIONS

Place each chicken breast half between 2 sheets of wax paper. Flatten them to ¼-inch thickness, using a meat mallet or rolling pin. Combine oil and next 3 ingredients in a zip-top heavy-duty plastic bag. Add chicken and marinate for 1 hour. Remove chicken from marinade (reserve). Sprinkle chicken with salt and pepper. Grill chicken, covered, over medium coals 7 minutes on each side, basting twice with the reserved marinade. Garnish. Salute Dolly Parton.

---

we got to the cue, he held up both hands and mouthed, "Stop!"

I stopped. I was puzzled, but I stopped in mid-word. Then he mouthed, "Okay," and motioned with his hands for me to continue. I continued to the end.

Harry said, "Cut," the sound man held his thumb up, Harry nodded to the assistant director who said, "That's a print. Coming around on Burt's single."

I didn't know why it worked this time, but I knew that somehow Burt had saved my bacon. I walked over to thank him, and he explained what had happened. We took a little walk and he told me about overlap. It's a term used in editing. You have to leave a little space for the editors to be able to edit the scene the way the director envisions it. I was doing exactly the opposite. I told him I was dumb for not asking. He said no, that would be an admission of lack of experience. I said I guessed I had a lot to learn. He agreed and graciously gave me some tips. Here are a few:

Burt Reynolds's Tips to Stardom

1. Never accept a cup of coffee from an extra. They are jealous of you, and they will pee in it.

2. Try to avoid speaking to anyone. It's all right to talk to stuntmen but make it quick.

3. It is important to look pissed off all the time. Kick pebbles.

4. If a phone is handy, pretend to be screaming at your agent. Say things like, "I don't care what Jack Warner says. It's a million bucks or no dice."

5. If you bring your script to the set, fill it full of handwritten notes with lots of the script marked out or underlined several times. Make sure it is rolled up.

6. If someone sits in your set chair, choke them until they are unconscious.

I didn't catch on that he was pulling my leg until "kick pebbles." We were immediate friends from that moment on. Without Burt, this would be a very short book.

Burt would frequently run an idea by me and often we agreed together about what he should or shouldn't do. We were doing *The Rainmaker* together in Chicago, and Burt told me that he had been approached by *Cosmopolitan Magazine* to do a foldout for women of the same sort *Playboy* did for men. Both of us thought it would be a hoot. However, Dinah Shore, who Burt was dating at the time, and Burt's publicity person weren't so sure. They thought he should let somebody else be first and see how it went from there. I disagreed and said so. I argued that nobody would ever remember who the second or third guy was that did a male nude foldout for *Cosmo*. I also thought he should only agree if he could pick the photo. After all, this was a parody of *Playboy* and other men's magazines, and it should appear that way.

I forgot all about it until a few months later when I got a frantic call from Burt. He was once again in Chicago and he wanted me to meet him there and fly with him to New York, where he was the guest host of *The Tonight Show*. The *Cosmo* with the foldout had gone on the stands that morning and had sold out in two hours. He said the phone wouldn't stop ringing, and he needed my help. I took the

On stage with Burt Reynolds in *The Rainmaker* at The Arlington Park Theatre. *Author Collection.*

next flight to Chicago. When I got there, Burt was a wreck. He was right. The phone never stopped ringing. I took messages while he got dressed and we left for New York.

On the flight, Burt showed me a letter from his publicist urging him not to go on the show at all. Dinah and the publicist were afraid he would be the laughingstock of the country. They were sure he was in danger of ruining his career. He thought they were wrong, and so did I. I told him he should tell all the jokes on himself first and everyone would know he did it for fun.

The *Tonight Show* had plenty of good writers, but none of them knew him like I did, so I told him what I would do if I were he.

"When you are introduced by Ed McMahon, wait a few beats before you come out from behind the curtain. When you do start to come out, do it as an old-time burlesque dancer. Tease the audience as they always did. Pull the lapel of your sports coat off your shoulder and have Doc Severinsen strike up 'The Stripper.' When you sit down with Ed, have him ask you why you did it. You tell him this story.

"'Years ago, way out west, there was a cowboy named Tex who got real drunk after a cattle drive, stripped buck naked, ran out into the desert, and jumped on a cactus.'

"Later, as the doc was pulling cactus thorns out of Tex's hide, he asked him, 'Tex, why in tarnation did you do such a dang-fool thing?' Tex replied, 'I dunno. It seemed like a good idea at the time!'"

Burt and I were right. Everybody got the joke. Men and women loved him for it. That night at the hotel, I screened his calls. Gloria Steinem called to tell Burt that he had struck a blow for women. It was a wild, crazy, exhilarating night.

My favorite call was from Jack Benny. His voice was unmistakable. Burt took the phone and in seconds was rolling with laughter. After he hung up he told me Jack wanted him to be on his next TV special. I wanted to know what made him laugh so hard.

Burt mimicked Jack's voice perfectly, "Burt, this is Jack Benny . . . I know a couple of things about timing . . . . you see what I mean? And you were brilliant tonight!"

DORIS DAY

Did I mention I was lucky?

Hot off the heels of *F Troop*, my agent proudly proclaimed that we had managed to snag a role on a new television show that was sure to be a hit. Oh, and by the way, the star was Doris Day.

Who doesn't love Doris Day? I was absolutely crazy about her and those great films she made with so many wonderful leading men like David Niven, Rock Hudson, and my pal James Garner. Her pipes weren't bad either. I'm not sure how many people these days know it, but she started out as a singer in the 1940s working with the likes of Bob Crosby and Les Brown. She hit the high mark in every genre from music to movies to television, being nominated for and winning Grammy Awards, Golden Globe Awards, and Academy Awards, not to mention the Presidential Medal of Freedom.

I was equally excited and intimidated by the prospect of working with her, so much so that it made me want to throw up on my shoes. What if she thought I was a complete dope? After all, at that point in my career, my resume was probably shorter than her grocery list. Actually, I couldn't figure out why she was doing the show at all. Back then not many actors of her stature would have unless it was some sort of television special. I

Doris and me, "LeRoy B. Simpson." *Courtesy of Pierre Patrick and BearManor Media.*

later learned that her late husband and manager, Martin Melcher, had, before his unexpected death, committed her to do it without her knowledge. He had also, along with their lawyer, robbed her blind. So, she did what we would have expected Doris Day to do; she marched on with her head held high and proceeded to take over the Nielsen ratings.

The first actor I ran into on the set was Denver Pyle. He played Doris's father on the show, and he put me at ease right away. He was always fun to be around, and we both liked to play cards during breaks in shooting. Denver also directed some of the episodes and was a terrific director. In the years to come, we would go on to work together on *Hawmps!* and *The Dukes of Hazzard*.

The premise of the show was that Doris was a widow who moved back to the family farm with her two kids. The boys who played Doris's sons, Todd Starke and Philip

Brown, were wonderful kid actors. Todd passed away too young, in a motorcycle accident, but Philip has had a long career and become a very familiar face on television. He's still acting today.

Doris, or Dodo as she asked me to call her, was indeed America's Sweetheart. She was gorgeous, down to earth, generous, and talented. She was in her mid-forties when she did *The Doris Day Show*, but she looked all of twenty-five to me, with a smile that would knock your socks off. Can you hear my heartbeat?

She was already a crusader for animals back then, and it seemed like there were always a lot of them on the set, including one of the show's costars, the Old English sheepdog, Lord Nelson. One week, we had a script that involved a tiger—a real live tiger. With real live teeth. Gigantic, gnashing, Jimmy Hampton-eating teeth. The story was that the tiger was a tame runaway, and my

The Doris Day Show cast. *Courtesy of Pierre Patrick and BearManor Media.*

character, the farm's handyman, Leroy B. Simpson, and Doris's character had to try to capture it before it was to be killed by the authorities. Most of the time, my knees were shaking so bad that I was surprised they didn't shoot me from the waist up. Ever hear the old adage that animals can smell fear? I was reeking—but not Dodo. To her that tiger may as well have been a kitten. Add fearless to her list of attributes.

I left the show after the first season but with no hard feelings. They simply changed the storyline, taking Doris's character into the city. So there was no longer a need for a bumbling handyman. I did do several episodes in the second season, including two in which the plot revolved around my character, Leroy.

Doris called me several years ago with the release of the first *The Doris Day Show* DVD and we continued to correspond every so often until she passed away at ninety-seven. I'm glad this world had her for as long as it did.

Besides my friendships with Doris and Denver, the best thing I took away from my experience on *The Doris Day Show* was a new love—for rocky road ice cream. It was Doris's favorite, and after she gave me my first scoop, it's been mine, too, ever since. I think of her every time I have a bowl. Thanks, Dodo.

CBS promo shot for *The Doris Day Show. Courtesy of Pierre Patrick and BearManor Media.*

Did I mention I love ice cream? *Author Collection.*

Rocky Road Ice Cream Pie, A La Doris Day

Thank you, DODO!

INGREDIENTS FOR THE CRUST

1 ½ cups graham cracker crumbs
3 tablespoons sugar
⅓ cup butter
Combine all 3 ingredients, press into pie pan, and bake at 325 degrees for 10 minutes. Cool completely.

INGREDIENTS FOR THE FILLING

½ gallon Rocky Road ice cream (Blue Bell is my favorite), slightly softened

1 cup cold heavy whipping cream and 2-4 tablespoons of powdered sugar, whipped together
Chocolate shavings

NOTE: Be sure the bowl you whip the whipping cream in is very cold

DIRECTIONS

Fill prepared graham cracker crust with ice cream. Top with whipped cream and chocolate shavings.

Cook's suggestion: Don't tell anyone you made this and eat it all yourself!

CLINT EASTWOOD

I came very close to never meeting Clint Eastwood. It certainly was miraculous that I was ever cast in an episode of *Rawhide*, the highly acclaimed series that established Clint's career. It all happened as a result of the generosity of spirit of a complete stranger.

Directly across the street from the main gate from what is now known as CBS-Radford Studios, was a little bar/eatery that was a favorite spot for a quick drink and a hamburger. I'm sure the place had a regular name, but everybody referred to it as "The Black and Blue Room," in reference to the fights that broke out there at regular intervals. Nothing too serious—usually just a misunderstanding between some good ol' boys who had been over-served. Bill, the owner, was an ex-stuntman from Oklahoma who could keep things from getting too out of hand, aided by a small bat he kept behind the bar. If you were celebrating, it was a good place to end up after you had overstayed your welcome at some of the more discriminating saloons along Ventura Boulevard. Best of all, if you were tapped, Bill would carry your tab till payday.

Dropping in for lunch, your entrance would be cut short until your eyes adjusted to the darkness. It was similar to coming out of bright sunshine and into the neighborhood movie house on a Saturday afternoon, except the pleasant aroma of fresh popcorn was replaced by the odors of stale beer, Marlboros, and onions on the grill. On the old Wurlitzer jukebox in the corner, Patsy Cline would be falling to pieces, or Johnny Cash would be walking the line. Using the glow from the neon beer signs, and following the sounds of coughing, you could navigate past the pool table and find some pals at the bar. It should also be noted that Bill made the best chili west of El Paso, without beans or tomato sauce, which as any civilized person knows is the way God meant for us to eat chili. Plus, they had Michelob on tap, and Bill would cash your unemployment check.

I had dropped by the Black and Blue Room one night for a cool one or three. I guess I was just looking for some company. I was a little bit homesick, a little bit lonesome, and more than a little bit loaded. I spotted a script supervisor I knew waving me over to a corner booth, where she was having drinks with some friends. She introduced me to everyone and invited me to join the crowd. She was sitting next to a guy I had never seen before who, I thought, was giving me the get-lost look. He pointed out that I had a Texas drawl (which was more pronounced

when I drank) and made a comment about it, which I ignored. I noticed, however, that he had an Irish accent and appeared to be a little drunk. He seemed to be spoiling for a fight and directed another sarcastic remark towards me that had just a little too much of an edge.

Then I said something really stupid.

"You seem to be quite an entertaining guy there, Mickey. How about doing us a nice Irish jig?"

We dived across the table at each other. Some punches were thrown, but cooler heads prevailed, and a friend drove me home.

The following day, my agent called me in the middle of my hangover to tell me I had a meeting that morning with the producers of *Rawhide*. There was a good role that had become available at the last minute, and it would begin shooting the next day. My head was throbbing as I took down the information. I had less than an hour to shave, dress, and get over there. I was happy about the audition. I just wished I felt better. *Rawhide* was shot at CBS-Radford, and the producer's office was on the lot. I needed to go by there anyway to pick up my car, as it was still in the parking lot across the street. I shaved, dressed hurriedly, and took a cab to the studio. I was still a little woozy as I climbed the stairs to the producer's office. Once more, I reminded myself of the perils of vodka and tonic on an empty stomach.

The show was produced by the talented writer/producer team of Bernie Kowalski and Bruce Geller. I had been trying to get my agents at the Kohner office to get me in to see them, as they produced other shows in addition to *Rawhide*. I entered the outer waiting room, signed in at the receptionist's desk, picked up the portion of the script with my name on it, and joined a few other actors who were studying their sides. I began to read the scene I was to audition for. It was the role of a townie who was applying for a job as a drover. I should be able to relate to that, I thought, as I was indeed in that office applying for a job.

Presently I was ushered into the office where I was introduced to Bruce, Bernie, and the director, Michael O'Herlihy. I froze in my tracks. My mouth went dry and my tongue began to swell. As I shook the hand of the director, and his eyes met mine, I recognized the face of the man I had asked to do an Irish jig the night before. I was sunk. I knew what was coming next and I deserved it.

Without the slightest hesitation Michael said, "Oh yes, of course. I'm familiar with Mr. Hampton's work. There is

A mouth bigger than mine! *Author Collection.*

no need for him to read. He'll be ideal for the role."

Suddenly his abrasive, Irish accent from the night before became a lovely, lilting Irish brogue. *What a lovely man this Michael is*, I thought.

Bruce looked a little surprised but shook my hand and said, "Well, welcome aboard."

I had an early call, so I had studied my lines and gone to bed at a reasonable hour. I arrived on the set early after going to makeup and wardrobe. Coffee from the catering truck in hand, and tissue around my collar so as not to soil my shirt with pancake makeup, I strolled around my new surroundings. As I walked around the Western town set where the morning work was to take place, I marveled at the skill of the set designers. The dusty streets, wooden sidewalks, and hitching rails with horses tied to them were completely authentic. There were shops, saloons, a bank, and even a newspaper office. When it was Republic Studios, hundreds of "oaters" had been filmed right where I was standing.

I was looking forward to meeting Clint Eastwood, as my pal Burt Reynolds had mentioned that Clint was a good guy. Women seemed to be crazy about him, but I thought he was a little skinny.

The first assistant director rounded up the participants for the first scene, and we assembled in front of the general store. There were about twenty or so actors and extras, and we were given our places in line. There was a table and chair for Rowdy Yates, Clint's character, who was hiring us townsfolk to be drovers for the herd.

We were not rehearsing lines at this point, merely setting up the opening scene, which would include a panning shot to establish where we were and continuing down the line of men looking for work, finally landing on Clint/Rowdy. Only Clint wasn't in his chair. I thought that was a bit odd. We were all on our marks, but Clint's stand-in was in the chair. The first assistant director told the actors to relax in the canvas set chairs that had been placed in a circle nearby. Our director, Michael, called us together, and we began to run lines for the hiring scene. Clint showed up about this time looking a lot like I had felt the day before. He was rumpled and unshaven, his eyes were bloodshot, and it was apparent (to me anyway) that he had really tied one on. Michael called action for the rehearsal, and we began. Clint mumbled, yawned, and stretched his way through what I felt was a very unsatisfactory rehearsal. Nevertheless, I had done my best. Michael seemed very upbeat in spite of Clint's disinterest in the work.

I was beginning to get pissed. My inner dialogue said, *Listen pal, this may be old stuff for you—you're a regular on the show and a big hit with the girls—but this is my only shot and I would appreciate it if you would give it your best.*

I think Michael had noticed that I was getting upset because I had shot him a glance or two when Clint was mumbling almost incoherently during the rehearsal. Michael looked amused as he walked over my way. I hadn't approached him, because I was so embarrassed at what I had done in the bar, I hoped there would be no references to that night. There weren't. Michael never, ever brought it up. Instead he sat down and very quietly offered several options for my character and some wonderful suggestions. He didn't insist on any of them, but it was clear he knew more about my character than I did. I was immediately calmed, and the notion of chastising Clint vanished in my growing admiration for Michael as a director and a human being. In the several shows I had done, there were few directors who took the precious time that is available in television production to direct actors at all.

Soon it was time to reassemble for the filming of the scene. We all took our places, found our key lights and our marks, and submitted to makeup giving us final pats with powder puffs. Action was called, and the scene began. To my dismay, Clint was doing it exactly like he did in the rehearsal. He was yawning, staring off into space, and exhibiting complete disinterest in what he was doing. I was flabbergasted! I even had to lean in a couple of times to hear his lines. I looked at some of the other actors as if to say, *What's with this guy anyway? He is just going through the motions.*

Then, it hit me. Oh . . . My . . . God. I remembered the setup for the beginning of the show. It was all in the script that I had given a cursory glance to. Rowdy was up half the night having drinks with the boys, playing cards, and spending time with the ladies. He was awakened out of a sound sleep and told to go hire some guys to move the herd. Rowdy does what he's told, but he couldn't care less. He's sleepy, hungover, and tired. In other words, Clint played it exactly right. No wonder Michael was smiling. Clint had done it so naturally and convincingly that I had missed the point. He was acting all the time. It just didn't look like it. It never does with him.

Thanks for the lesson, Clint. And thank God, for once, I kept my mouth shut.

Rowdy Yates's Cowboy Pie

INGREDIENTS FOR THE FILLING

6 strips bacon, chopped

1 medium onion, chopped

1 pound ground beef

3 tablespoons parsley flakes

2 cloves garlic, crushed

1 teaspoon nutmeg

½ green bell pepper, finely chopped

1 teaspoon paprika

½ teaspoon thyme

1 15-ounce can tomato sauce

⅓ cup beer

1 16-ounce can whole corn

1 16-ounce bag frozen peas and carrots

2 tablespoons cornstarch blended with 2 tablespoons cold water

Salt and pepper to taste

INGREDIENTS FOR CORNMEAL TOPPING

1 ½ cups cornmeal

1 cup flour

1 teaspoon baking soda

3 teaspoons baking powder

1 teaspoon salt

2 tablespoons sugar

2 eggs

1 cup beer

1 cup buttermilk

¼ cup oil

1 ½ cups grated cheddar cheese

DIRECTIONS

Preheat oven to 400 degrees. Butter or spray a large baking dish. In a saucepan, combine bacon, onion and ground beef. Cook over medium heat until meat is well browned. Add remaining ingredients except for the corn, peas and carrots and cornstarch mixture. Allow to simmer 10 to 20 minutes so flavors meld. Stir in cornstarch mixture and heat a few minutes more. Stir in corn and frozen peas and carrots and transfer filling to a baking dish.

In a medium bowl, combine the dry ingredients for the cornmeal topping. Add liquid ingredients for the cornmeal topping and mix well. Fold in grated cheese. Pour cornmeal batter over the prepared meat filling. Bake for 30 to 40 minutes until topping is golden brown and knife inserted comes out clean.

Yeeeeeeee Haaaaaaaw!!!

EFREM ZIMBALIST JR.

Efrem Zimbalist had everything you ever wanted to find in a big star: intelligence, kindness, charisma, and talent, to name just a few of his assets. He was also funny, charming, and what we used to call a well-bred gentleman. I met Efrem when I was cast as a bad guy on his television series *The F.B.I.* I was very interested in expanding my image as the antagonist on detective shows because there were quite a few roles available for actors who could play against type. That meant that an actor like me, with a good guy image, could provide the audience with a level of surprise when it was revealed that it was the supposed good guy who was actually the criminal. I was mildly successful in this area for a few years. For some reason, I became a kidnapper several times (*Mannix, Manhunter,* and others), but to my dismay, I never got to murder anybody. Murderers get the real money.

Nevertheless, I had some ideas about how I wanted to play a bad guy. My first idea was that bad guys don't believe they are bad. They think they are misunderstood perhaps, but not really bad. I liked the way Richard Widmark, Dan Duryea, and Fred MacMurray had all played bad guys, always smiling and full of charm until they did something really mean. They never even had raised their voices. Widmark seemed to think that pushing a paraplegic down the stairs was riotously funny. There was no doubt they were enjoying themselves.

My second idea about bad guys was that they didn't run fast enough. The thing that drove me nuts was the way they did foot chases in movies. They just didn't look like they were running fast enough to really get away. For instance, they would run into an alley, stop, look confused, decide which way to run, and take off again. Total elapsed screen time: ten seconds, including a close-up. Moments later, the detective good guy shows up, stops, looks confused, then for no apparent reason trots off in the correct direction at a leisurely pace.

Whenever I watched this scenario unfold as a kid, I would always think to myself, *My grandmother could outrun those guys!* I vowed to myself in that darkened theater on that particular Saturday morning that if I ever became an actor and I had an opportunity to escape from the law as a bad guy, I would run as hard and as fast as I could. There was such an opportunity in that *The F.B.I.* episode.

On the morning we were slated to film the chase scene, I marched up to the director and tried to sell him on my idea. I told him about how I felt regarding the chase scenes

With Mike Connors in *Mannix. Author Collection.*

I had seen as a kid. I told him about my vow. I told him I wanted to run. I wanted to run *fast*. I wanted to run as fast as I could, and I wanted to really try to get away.

He looked at me for a moment, smiled, and said, "Fine with me. You might want to run it by Efrem."

Then he turned to the director of photography.

"We're going to need a lot of track."

I was over the first hurdle. I waited patiently for Mr. Zimbalist to arrive on the set.

My first impression of Efrem was of an extremely congenial and handsome man who would look right at home with a cashmere sweater tied around his neck and a tennis racquet in his hand. Instead he had a cup of coffee and a donut. I approached him as he was smiling and greeting members of the crew. It was the seventh year of that very successful series, and everyone was relaxed and friendly. I introduced myself and he put the donut in his mouth, shook my hand, and welcomed me to the show. He was very genuine and made me feel a part of the cast. After a few pleasantries the director and the director of photography came over. They were all old friends and glad to see each other. The director spoke.

"Jim's got an interesting idea. Did you tell him yet, Jim?"

I hadn't, so I did. I told him I wanted to really run. I told him why I wanted to run. I made it clear I would do my best to actually get away. It sounded a little dorky coming out of my mouth again, but I thought Efrem looked intrigued.

"Well, I think that's a fine idea. Splendid!"

He turned to the director.

"Where do you want me to catch him?"

The director indicated a spot a few yards from where we were standing. Efrem nodded and turned his attention to his donut and coffee. I was puzzled. Could he have misunderstood?

The director told me I would have about an eight-yard head start. Efrem looked fit, but so was I. I was thirty-six and he was fifty-two. That's eighteen years! I mean, come on.

It took another half hour or so for the shot to be set up. There must have been half a football field of track the grips were laying. A couple of guys would be pushing a camera dolly on a track with three persons on it and a big heavy camera. I was getting sick to my stomach. This was a terrible idea. The guys that were going to be pushing looked a little overweight. They were having a smoke. *What if one of them has a heart attack? It would be all my fault.* Maybe we should just do it the old way where I run into an alley and look confused in my close-up. I was about to hurl when the first assistant director came over to tell me we were about five minutes away and to check with makeup because I looked a little pale.

It was time for the shot. I had made my bed. I was going to have to run in it, so to speak. I went over to Efrem. He was in wardrobe, wearing a suit with a tie and ordinary businessman's street shoes. *Poor bastard*, I thought. I felt bad for him. *Maybe we should forget the whole thing.*

"Remember, Efrem. I'm going to try to get away. Really."

"Yeah, I know. Great!"

I looked down at my tennis shoes. *Okay, I tried to warn them.*

"Roll film. Speed. Action!"

I was off like a gazelle. It was like running downhill. I didn't look back. It wasn't my fault.

Maybe I'll make the highlight reel for bloopers! The one that got away from Lew Erskine of The F.B.I.!

A few more yards and I would be at the finish line where the director told Efrem he would like the arrest to take place. One more step and . . . wham! A hand had reached out, grabbed me by the collar, expertly used my own force to spin me around and up against a wall (funny, I didn't remember seeing that before). My legs were spread, and my hands cuffed behind me while Inspector Erskine read me my rights without even breathing hard. Cut, print, and bring up the theme music.

I turned my head around just far enough to see the two dolly grips lighting up another Marlboro and giving each other high fives.

As I was being helped to my chair by the property master who was getting me out of my handcuffs, I heard Efrem say, "Great idea, Jim. That was fun."

ADRIENNE BARBEAU

Adrienne Barbeau saved my life. I mean that literally. This is how it happened. Burt Reynolds and I were doing a picture in Nashville called *W. W. and the Dixie Dancekings*. It had a wonderful cast headed by Art Carney, Conny Van Dyke, Jerry Reed, Rick Hurst, and many others. The director was John Avildsen, who went on to direct *Rocky*, which earned him an Oscar. Burt loved Nashville and he was in awe of the gigantic pool of talent in the music industry there, so much so that he even cut a country-and-western album while we were doing the picture. I'd love to hear it sometime.

Burt and I roomed together whenever we could on location. He didn't like hotels as much as the privacy afforded by a fully furnished home rental. For me, I really liked to have a kitchen with a completely stocked refrigerator. Burt also had a bigger problem. Once the fans found him in a hotel, and they always did, the chances of getting any rest were almost nonexistent.

The studio found a really nice three-bedroom house in a secluded, wooded area on the outskirts of Nashville.

It was a split-level with a complete kitchen and a full fridge. I was happy. My bedroom, on the lowest level, had a beautiful view with a terrace. I could play my Elton John *Yellow Brick Road* album as loud as I wanted. As a surprise bonus from Fox, our transportation was a brand-new yellow Corvette.

One of the things I admired about Burt was his attitude towards his celebrity. He had a nice career going for him and his star was definitely rising, but he remained the same good ol' boy I had met on *Gunsmoke*. On the day that it was reported in *Variety* that he was the number-four box-office name in the world, we celebrated by driving around Nashville in the 'vette, harassing cars full of girls. We would pull up beside them at a red light and he would lean out the window and yell, "Hey! Guess what? I'm number four in the world!" Their shocked expressions would cause us to cackle like high school sophomores while we sped off down the road looking for more victims.

Burt was having fun and he made himself available to

CUDDLE AT CONFAB. "We can't go on meeting like this" joke Jim Hampton and Maude's Adrienne Barbeau as our photog catches them at Actor's Guild session.

Sharing a hug with the beautiful Adrienne Barbeau.
Author Collection.

the public in many ways. One of those ways was appearing on telethons. As it happened, there was a star-studded telethon in Nashville benefiting some worthwhile charity, and Burt decided it would be a grand idea to go. One of the things Burt enjoyed about being famous was an opportunity to meet other famous people, especially musicians and singers, and Nashville was full of them. That night, apart from all the wonderful, talented country-and-western stars, there were TV stars, and for me, the biggest star of all was the "Godfather of Soul," James Brown! It was a fabulous night. When James Brown was onstage, I couldn't resist joining him and mimicking all of his famous dance moves. I have never seen anyone laugh as hard as James did and we brought the place down. I staggered offstage to find some oxygen, and Adrienne Barbeau took over. This girl could really dance! We became lifelong friends on the spot.

Adrienne liked cooking as much as I did. She was Armenian and could cook with spices producing aromas and tastes that are indescribable. She volunteered to make dinner for Burt and me, which we readily accepted. She got a ride over in the late afternoon and arrived with sacks full of interesting grocery items. We had an eight o'clock call that evening and left the kitchen to her. We decided

that we would have a late dinner around midnight. We had a night scene to shoot outside of the Orchid Lounge, but it didn't look like it would take more than a couple of hours. I was looking forward to that dinner even though I was experiencing a little heartburn. I had noticed it off and on for a few days and had a bottle of Pepto Bismol in the motorhome/dressing room on set that Burt and I shared.

It was one of those nights that sometimes happen when you are on location making a movie—everything went wrong. We didn't even get started until after midnight. John Avildsen was a very patient man and the sort of director to persevere until everything is done to his liking. We hung in there, Burt drinking black coffee while I sipped on Pepto.

Finally, we wrapped at ten minutes till three in the morning. When we got back, we just wanted to crash. As we opened the door, a wonderful aroma of fine Armenian cuisine met us. We had totally forgotten Adrienne's dinner! Not that we could have done anything about it. There were no cell phones in those days. She had left a note on the beautifully set dining-room table saying that she had guessed what was happening, took one of the bedrooms, and gone to bed. At the bottom of the note was a postscript: "Burt, I swiped one of your shirts."

After we gorged ourselves, Burt took a sleeping pill, and I took the last of the Pepto and tiptoed downstairs where I fell immediately to sleep. I woke two hours later to the most severe pain I had ever experienced. It was no mere heartburn, no mere queasy stomach, or even cramps. It was a piercing, searing, relentless pain which had moved down almost to my right groin. I tried to get out of bed but could not. The pain was so awful I couldn't sit upright and swing my feet to the floor. I managed to turn on my right side and scoot off the bed. I knew immediately what it was—appendicitis. I needed to get to a hospital. I reached over to the nightstand and got my wallet. I knew I would need an insurance card. I had gone to bed in a T-shirt and boxer shorts. That would have to do.

I began to crawl. Every movement was agony. I got through the door and began climbing up the stairs. What seemed like hours was probably only a few minutes. Finally, I was outside of Burt's bedroom. I opened the door and crawled over to the bed. I tried to rouse him, but the sleeping pill had knocked him out. Suddenly he woke.

"Whasamatter?"

"I've got appendicitis. I gotta get to a hospital."

He seemed to try to process this information. Finally, he spoke.

"Take some Pepto and go back to bed."

With that, he fell straight back and was out cold. I noticed the car keys on the bedside table. I got them and started crawling out the door. It was no good. Even if I could make it to the car, I couldn't possibly drive. Then I remembered that Adrienne was right across the hall. I managed to get myself out into the hallway, hoping Adrienne had only borrowed Burt's shirt and not his sleeping pills. I opened the door with my last ounce of strength.

"Adri!" I was spent.

She sat bolt upright in bed and, unlike Burt, she was completely awake and alert.

There is a god, I thought.

In that split second, I was at peace. If this was the last sight I would ever gaze upon, I was ready to go. She had neglected to button the shirt.

"Jimmy! What's the matter?"

"Appendicitis."

She was up in a flash—no questions, all business. She was dressed and helping me to the car in seconds. Somehow, with her help, I was able to contort myself into the Corvette's passenger seat.

"Uh oh," she said.

"What uh oh?"

"I don't know how to drive a stick shift."

"Put the key into the ignition. I'll tell you what to do."

I put the gear shift into neutral. We started. After a few failed attempts, we got the car out of the driveway. She was encouraged.

"Okay. Where's the hospital?"

I realized I had no idea. I then took inventory of the situation. In the predawn hours on the remote outskirts of Nashville, we had a guy whose appendix was about to rupture, a beautiful Armenian actress who hadn't a clue how to drive a race car, and neither knew how to get to the city, let alone to a hospital. Not good.

Then I noticed a glow in the distance.

"Head towards the light."

We ended up driving in second gear, but we made it to the emergency room where a fine surgeon told me my appendix would have burst in less than half an hour. Then they gave me something for the pain. When I woke up, I was lying comfortably in the Tammy Wynette Suite at Baptist Hospital.

Some people left their hearts in San Francisco . . . I left my appendix in Nashville. Thanks to Adrienne, Burt, Tammy, General Motors, and Dr. Goldberg (who wishes to remain anonymous).

I lost my appendix in Nashville while shooting *W. W. and the Dixie Dancekings. Author Collection.*

The cast of *W. W. and the Dixie Dancekings. Author Collection.*

Adrienne Barbeau "What a Honey" Cake

INGREDIENTS

3 eggs
1 cup sugar
1 cup honey
1 cup brewed black coffee
2 teaspoons baking powder
1 teaspoon baking soda
1 teaspoon ginger
1 teaspoon nutmeg
1 teaspoon cinnamon
3 ¼ cups all-purpose flour

2 Tablespoons chopped nuts
Additional chopped nuts for bottom of pan
2 Tablespoons canola oil

DIRECTIONS

Beat eggs well, adding sugar gradually. Mix in honey and coffee. Sift together remaining dry ingredients. Add oil, sifted dry ingredients, and nuts to the beaten egg mixture. Sprinkle bottom of greased tube pan with nuts. Pour in dough. Bake at 350 degrees for 40 minutes. Let cool, flip over, and sift powdered sugar over the top.

FORREST TUCKER

The first time I saw Forrest Tucker he was nursing a Dewar's on the rocks, sitting in his *F Troop* golf cart, made up, wardrobed, and ready to go. At six-foot-five and 240 pounds, he looked very much The Star. We shook hands and he immediately made the following observation:

"Damn son! If your eyes were any closer together, they'd be in single file!"

It caught me off guard, and I laughed as hard as I ever have. It certainly broke the ice and I felt welcome. He offered me a seat in the cart and a drink, but I declined the drink. It was 6:30 in the morning.

His specially made golf cart was amazing. It had a bar with liquor and an ice chest, and a small TV set, and was decorated with cavalry sabers and even a bugle.

Tuck lived about two and a half blocks from one of the gates at Warner Brothers Studios where *F Troop* was filmed. About a block from his modest apartment was the entrance to the Lakeside Country Club, home to every actor from W. C. Fields and *Tarzan's* Johnny Weissmuller to Bing Crosby and Oliver Hardy. Tuck claimed that everything he wanted or needed was within that quarter-mile radius. It was his kingdom.

Later that first day of filming, a group of nuns began filing in just as Tuck was regaling us with stories about some of the biggest names in Hollywood at the time. He was very entertaining and had a booming, gravelly voice which was no doubt enhanced by the ever-present Camel cigarette in his hand. At that moment, Tuck's stand-in, who had studied for the priesthood, came

With pal Forrest Tucker. *Author Collection.*

over to alert Tuck to the presence of the good sisters. The stand-in's concern was for Tuck's language. Tuck, slightly miffed at the interruption in the middle of a good story, wheeled around and spotted the nuns on the other side of the set.

Without skipping a beat or lowering his Irish baritone, Tuck uttered, "Screw 'em! They got their racket and I got mine!"

You'll have to admit he had a point. It was his domain they were invading, not the safety of the abbey. In spite of his sometimes rough language, Tuck had many good qualities. Not the least of these was his total honesty.

He was a consummate professional; he was never late on the set and he always knew his lines. However, even under the best circumstances there are times when we would have to wait until everything was ready. Some of us would nap, play cards, or swap stories. Larry would read or sunbathe; Ken would work on a new step for his tap routine; and Melody would go to school. It was Tuck's habit, when he was waiting for his time at bat, to sit in his cart, sip scotch, and enjoy life.

Once, late in the day, while he never missed his mark or blew his lines, there was an accident while performing a bit of business with Dobbs the bugler (me).

Hannibal Dobbs was a terrible bugler, but he was unaware of that fact. Occasionally, there were times when he needed to be silenced in one way or another. Most of his comrades tried to break it to him gently except for Corporal Agarn, who was in the habit of smacking Dobbs with his hat. In the script we were performing that day, it was indicated that Sergeant O'Rourke would simply cover the bell of the horn with one of his hands. Unfortunately, instead of doing what was rehearsed, Tuck thought it would be funnier if he banged the end of the bugle in exasperation. Not knowing what was coming, I was unprepared. The result was that he knocked out one of my teeth. I was so surprised and hurt, I realized I was about to crack him over the head with the bugle. But at that moment Tuck said, "Oh, you know I didn't mean to." He was right. I could see in his eyes he was slightly affected by the scotch but completely sincere in his apology.

Later he said to me, "Jim, were you really going to hit me with that bugle?"

I answered, "Well, I have to say, it certainly crossed my mind."

On one occasion, his plain language got him into a little trouble. During the auditions for the part of Wrangler Jane, the love interest for Ken Berry's Captain Parmenter, the actresses were told they must be at least eighteen years old. Melody Patterson was chosen, and her mother swore she was eighteen. I'm sure she must have thought that the show would never air, and Melody might as well do the pilot. After the show was picked up by ABC, we all learned she was, in fact, only sixteen years of age! Our producer, Hy Averback, was furious—Melody was so good in the role. She could ride a horse at full gallop, and she was beautiful! A compromise was drawn: Melody had to finish high school, so a teacher was hired.

(Staff photo by John Foster)

STARS OF 'F TROOP' REHEARSE FOR NIGHT CLUB ACT . . from left, Larry Storch, Forrest Tucker, Ken Barry, Jim Hampton

Tuck was amused by all this and decided to make a joke about her age at the read-through.

When Melody arrived Monday morning, he greeted her by asking, "Did you get laid yet?"

Then he laughed uproariously, and Melody blushed and was a good sport. It became a tradition on Mondays. "Did you get laid yet?" Eventually, the teacher had enough and complained about "inappropriate language," saying that if Tuck didn't stop, she would file a written complaint and there would be dire consequences. Poor Hy had to break the news to Tuck, who didn't take it very well. In fact, Tuck took umbrage toward any efforts to curtail his language.

In fact, Tuck took umbrage toward any efforts to curtail his blankety-blank first blankety-blank amendment and freedom of blankety-blank speech, and stormed out of the blankety-blank meeting. What would happen the following Monday was anybody's guess.

The day came. We were all assembled, and bets were made. Melody was the last one to appear. She was greeted by Hy, the writers, and the cast, except for Tuck. There wasn't a sound in the room apart from paper shuffling. Finally, Melody said, "Good morning everyone. Good morning, Mr. Tucker." Tuck smiled sweetly and leaned towards Melody. Then he said, "Good morning, Melody. How are things at the Cherry Festival?"

It was genius. All of us, including Hy, roared. Even the teacher hid her face. And so it was until *F Troop* was replaced by *The Flying Nun*.

There is another area I should deal with for the sake of history—Tuck's shlong. In the days before the internet,

With sweet Melody Patterson, 2001. *Author Collection.*

rumors were passed around in conversation. Sitting around waiting for the next shot is a perfect environment for gossip, especially celebrity gossip. Tuck, as the story went, was inordinately gifted in the penile area. Now, Ken Berry is a much nicer, more polite person than I am. He and I were both familiar with the story. We had heard that Tuck had once made a putt with his member, and I don't mean a member of the country club. One day when things were slow and the three of us were swapping stories, I winked at Ken, and asked Tuck if "The Story" was true. He smiled, took a sip of Dewar's, and told us. It was the ninth hole at Lakeside, a wicked par three of almost two hundred yards up a tree-lined incline to a wide but shallow green. There were several bets closing out the front nine, and Tuck was well ahead with an unpleasant man from out of town. Having the honors, he hit a perfect two iron with a little draw that was hunting the hole as soon as the ball left the club face. All who saw it knew it was good, but no one knew exactly how good until they arrived at the green.

Once they climbed the hill, they saw just how good it was. It was no more than eighteen inches away from the flag. It was, in golfing terms, a gimmie.

As Tuck walked over to pick up his Spaulding, he heard his opponent say, "Putt it." Tuck was astounded.

"What did you say?"

"Putt it."

"Come on. We've been giving these all day. It's in the leather."

"Putt it."

The man wasn't kidding.

Tuck was always a good sportsman as well as a superb golfer. The man, who was down perhaps a hundred dollars in bets by then, was trying to entice Tuck into losing his temper and thereby lose the hole. Tuck's Irish ire was rising. He knew that it was within the rules to putt all balls until holed, but not customarily practiced in gentlemen's golf.

Tuck looked hard at the man and said, "I can make this putt with my putz."

Without hesitation the man challenged, "For a hundred dollars."

At this point, Tuck got out of his cart and began to act out the rest of the story for me and Ken.

Tuck knelt on his right knee and said, "I got down on one knee, unzipped my fly, took out the Super Chief, and knocked that pretty little ball into the back of the cup."

The man from out of town vamoosed before paying up.

The following story about Tuck is a little bit different, but it's one that can be told in polite company. It's also my favorite.

We arrived at Stage Six at Warner Bros. about midway through the first year for the Monday morning table read. There was the usual joking around before we got down to business and plunged into the script. It was a good, funny show. We applauded when we finished.

Afterwards, Hy Averback routinely asked the cast if we had any problems with the script. Almost all of us thought it was a fine job and there were congratulations all around, except for Tuck. He was flipping pages like he was missing something.

"Just one thing, Hy, maybe it got skipped somehow, but I can't find Duffy in this script."

The character of Duffy was a cantankerous old trooper who was always shouting, "Remember the Alamo!" Bob Steele, the famous cowboy actor from the 1930s and 1940s, played the part.

For the first time that morning, I looked around and noticed that Bob was indeed missing.

Charming as ever, Hy smiled and said, "That's right. There just didn't seem anything for Duffy to do, so we wrote him out."

"Oh, I see. You wrote him out."

Tuck unfolded his six-foot-five frame and replied ever so sweetly.

"In that case, I will be at the bar at Lakeside. When Duffy is back in the script, give me a call."

Then he turned away, climbed into his electric cart, and drove away in the direction of Lakeside Country Club.

Hy was stunned speechless. So were we all. What

would we do now? After a minute or so, Hy said, "Take a smoke break, everyone. Don't go too far away. We will sort this out in a few minutes."

One of the writers was already on the phone. Actually, it took a few hours. We were sent home and didn't return to the set until Tuesday morning. We never started filming until Tuesday anyway, but occasionally on Mondays we would do some blocking on certain scenes. That evening, I got a new script delivered to my home. This one had a nice scene with Duffy in it.

Much later I found out what had happened. Early on, when the studio was courting Forrest for the *F Troop* role, big, tough guy Forrest Tucker had suggested to the producers and the powers that be that Bob Steele would be perfect for the part of Duffy. Tuck knew that Bob was struggling a bit and in need of a job. Bob, who at one time was the highest-paid actor in Hollywood, was too proud to use the influence of Tuck or anyone else to secure employment. But Forrest, who had suggested Bob Steele for the part, had one more ace in the hole. To their chagrin, when the lawyers took a look at Tuck's contract, they discovered that Bob Steele was to be in every episode of *F Troop*. Tuck was a good man to have in your corner.

Famous cowboy actor and *F Troop* castmate Bob Steele. *Author Collection.*

THE GATLIN BROTHERS

The Gatlin Brothers are not only great recording artists, they are also terrific golfers. It is no wonder they are invited to charity tournaments all over the map. Larry and Rudy are extroverts with wacky senses of humor, but Steve is The Quiet Gatlin.

Steve and I were relaxing in a hotel lobby after a round of golf, and we couldn't help but notice a big-bosomed blonde who was very animated, fueled by a few too many doses of Kentucky Loud Mouth. Every time she leaned over, she gave us an eyeful that turned grown men into little boys. We were speechless.

Steve turned to me and quietly said, "Jim, if that woman wants to sell those puppies, I'll take the one with the brown nose." Steve picks his moments, and then . . . ka-pow.

Oh, and Rudy, it's your turn to name a state.

Bo Hopkins, David Leisure, Mickey Jones, Casey Kasem, Pat Boone, and me in perfect harmony for charity. *Author Collection.*

BILLY BOB THORNTON

Quite simply, he's a genius.

I met Billy Bob when I was writing and directing *Evening Shade*. He had a couple of appearances on the show and was dynamite. So when Harry Thomason and

Linda Bloodworth-Thomason had an idea for a new sitcom called *Hearts Afire*, they cast him along with John Ritter, Markie Post, and my old friend from *Police Academy V*, George Gaynes. I ended up directing that show, and one day Billy Bob approached me about a role in a film he had written. He said he thought I'd be perfect for the character of Jerry Woolridge. He gave me the script, and I took it home. That evening, I picked it up and didn't put it down until I read the words "The End." I couldn't wait to accept his offer to appear in *Sling Blade*.

The picture was filmed for under a million dollars in several different locations in Arkansas, including Benton, which was near Malvern, where Billy Bob grew up. My dad, Ivan, was from Mena, and he and my mom had retired in Fort Smith. So, I was, in a 'round about way, a fellow Arkansan. It is still a place very near and dear to my heart.

On the set of *Sling Blade* with the brilliant Billy Bob Thornton. *Author Collection.*

Billy Bob had done a short of *Sling Blade* called *Some Folks Call It a Sling Blade*, but he decided on a mostly new cast for the full-length feature. What a cast. It was a remarkable ensemble of actors, some of whom were well-known like Robert Duvall, John Ritter, and J. T. Walsh, and some who were old veterans like me and Mickey Jones. There were also some first timers who were wonderful. As it turned out, his casting was also genius. We were nominated for Outstanding Performance By A Cast by the Screen Actors Guild in 1996. Unfortunately, we lost to the cast of *The Birdcage*. That same year *Sling Blade* was pitted against Miramax's

colossally big budget picture *The English Patient*, and while everyone thought *Sling Blade* should have won, it didn't. However, Billy Bob won the Oscar for Best Writing Adapted Screenplay. I couldn't tell you how many more honors he and the film received over the years, there were so many. But I will tell you this: watching *Sling Blade* touched my heart. Watching *The English Patient* only made me thirsty. Very, very, thirsty. If you've seen the first five minutes, you know what I mean.

Billy Bob once told me "I'd rather watch a small movie with a big story than a big movie with no story." I'm with you, kid. You hit it out of the ballpark.

GEORGE HAMILTON

George Hamilton was also a member of the *Cat Dancing* cast. George is an interesting and charming fellow who has spent a lot of time lying by the pool. He has an unusual sense of humor, and he doesn't take life very seriously. I like George, because more often than not, he has someone's leg and is pulling it like crazy.

Case in point: During the filming of *The Man Who Loved Cat Dancing*, Lee J. Cobb and George Hamilton had a bit of a falling out. To George, the script was something to refer to but ad-libbing was fine, not to mention fun. To Lee, a script was the Bible. It was old school against new school. Prankster George, as a joke, would rewrite the script the night before the next day's filming and slip it under Lee's door. The new pages cut out much of Lee's dialogue while adding to George's. Lee fell for it

hook, line, and sinker. When Lee asked director Richard Sarafian about the changes in the script, he didn't know what Lee was talking about. Lee was puzzled. Who would do such a thing?

Frankly, I thought it was pretty funny. George was just kidding around, but Lee didn't think staying up several hours trying to commit the new script to memory had a whole lot of humor to it.

When we boarded the bus to take us to the set, George, last to get on, yelled out to Lee, "Hey Lee, aren't these new changes great?"

The jig was up. Lee knew he had taken the bait and was reeled in. I sat next to him, and he didn't say a word on the trip to the locale. In any case, there was no love lost between them.

We were shooting a scene in front of a corral with a stallion and a couple of mares. It was awful. We did take after take, but something always happened. Usually it was something George did or didn't do. He reminded me of a little boy with attention deficit disorder. I believe he reminded Lee of a demon from hell. During a long speech by Lee, George kept flubbing his lines to Lee's mounting displeasure. Contrary to Lee, the stallion in the scene wasn't a trained actor. He began to lose his focus. Apparently, he was daydreaming about the time he had his way with a lovely Palomino and then began preparing for his duty. His shlong emerged.

When George saw the evidence the stallion was presenting, he (George) began to giggle and point saying, "Cut! Cut! Cut!"

This was the final blow.

There is an unwritten law that no one but the director can yell cut while filming.

Pointing at the horse, George, still laughing, declared, "I can't do a scene with one of those in it."

Ever so sweetly Lee replied, "Why not, George? I am!"

On the bus as we headed back to our showers, Mexican dinners, and cigars, Lee was a delightful and popular raconteur again. The same cast and crew so captivated by the Hamilton charm during the morning bus ride were now hanging on Cobb's every word. George, good natured to the end and gracious in defeat, came over and offered his hand.

"Well Lee, shall we bury the hatchet?"

"Certainly, George," he replied. "Bend over."

Game, set, match.

GEORGE LINDSEY

I met George on the set of a show called *The CBS Anthology.* I had seen him holding court with a few of the actors, and wherever George was, people were laughing. I could hear from his accent that he was from somewhere close to my neck of the woods. As it turned out, George was from Jasper, Alabama. One thing I know, when you meet someone from the South, you can cement your relationship by sharing some food, especially if it is Southern food.

I remembered I had a bag of salted in-the-shell peanuts that I got when I went to see the Dodgers play the night before. I went over to my set chair and grabbed the bag. Then I walked over to where George was and introduced myself. After we shook hands, I offered the peanuts.

"Would you like some peanuts?"

"No, thanks," George said, "I just had some soap."

I laughed so hard I had to be beaten on the back when I accidentally inhaled some peanut skins. To this day I have no idea what that meant, but it certainly caught me completely unawares. We were friends from that moment on.

He enjoyed a very successful and lucrative career. Probably one of his most memorable characters was that of Goober Pyle on *The Andy Griffith Show.* His character was not a Mensa candidate, but you would be wrong to assume that George was slow witted in any way. He was a university graduate with a degree in theater arts.

George went on to become part of the large cast on *Hee Haw* and is probably entertaining a group of people somewhere in Heaven right now. Here are a couple of his lines:

"I grew up in a house with three rooms and a path."

"Mama wrote me that a fire broke out in the bathroom, but they got it put out before it got to the house."

"Me and the wife have been married so long we're on our second bottle of Tabasco."

JACK GARNER

Jack Garner was probably the most gifted athlete I have ever known. Back in the day, a good high school athlete (particularly one from Oklahoma) would play all sports. Jack was outstanding at anything that included running, throwing, hitting, or kicking. In four years of high school

Jack accumulated some sixteen letters. He was the captain of state champions in basketball and football, but it was a baseball scout that signed him to a contract before he turned eighteen.

Jack was also a much sought-after teacher of the game.

He was an actor with a yard-long list of credits and a beautiful singing voice when harmonizing on Lyda Rose or Sweet Lorraine. Jack is the only person I have ever known who could sink a birdie putt while simultaneously whistling and smoking a Havana cigar. Well, I told you he was gifted. Oh yeah, his little brother Jim was kind of a famous actor too.

Jack had a gift of gab that charmed men and women alike, and he had one of the best pickup lines I ever heard. When he saw a pretty girl, he zeroed in like a heat-seeking missile.

"Hello there, Darling. Would you like to mess around?"

Naturally, his target was caught off guard and she would blush and stammer, "Certainly not!"

Undeterred, Jack would smile sweetly and close the deal.

"Well then, would you mind holding still while I do?"

Jack had an abundance of sports stories around from his years in the minor leagues. This is one of my favorites, as near as I can remember Jack telling it:

We were all loaded on the bus getting ready to go play a game in the Texas Panhandle. One of the young rookies got on and began walking down the aisle looking for a seat. He was a lefthander who was a little wild, but he had some heat on his fastball. All the good seats were already taken by regular players, but toward the back was an old outfielder who was sent down from the big leagues due to a nagging shoulder injury. He waved for the rook to sit by him, which was quite an honor for the kid. The old pro just wanted to be nice to the young man since he was pitching that night and was understandably nervous. The rookie thanked the older man, who then began a conversation with him.

"Say Meat, what are you doing tonight after the game?"

"Not much I guess. Probably get something to eat."

"Hey, I got an idea. Why don't we go chase some broads?"

"Well thanks . . . but I just couldn't do that."

"Why the hell not?"

The kid was starting to tremble a bit, and some of the guys were turning around from their card games to hear his answer.

"Well, I got a girlfriend back in Enid, and we're going to get married after the season's over. She made me promise to stay true to her and no other."

The outfielder considered this briefly, then exploded.

"Aw, that don't count! You name me one thing in the world as good as a roll in the hay with a pretty girl!"

The outfielder felt he had him. The other ballplayers were smiling and nodding. The old pro had made his point. The kid was beat, but he was a gamer. He wasn't giving up. He replied with a smile:

"Well . . . when I get up in the morning and have a cup of coffee, I like to sit on the toilet and read the sports section while I take a good crap."

JAMES ARNESS

The first time I ever saw James Arness was on the set of *Gunsmoke*. It was my first job in Hollywood, and I was dizzy with excitement. How I got the part is another story, but it was the guest-starring role on the number-one show in the nation. I had been a fan since the radio days, when the show was sponsored by Fatima cigarettes, with William Conrad as Matt Dillon and Parley Baer as Chester.

And there I was, amidst actors who had years of experience. I felt as though I was an imposter. At that precise moment, I heard some hearty laughter emanating from the craft services table. Back then I didn't know what it was, or that everything on it was free for the taking. I looked in that direction to see what was so riotously funny and saw Jim Arness, or more accurately, Matt Dillon.

Jim was in his marshal's getup: big hat, vest with a tin star, a big holstered six-shooter on his hip. He was holding his morning mug of coffee as he regaled some of the crew members. I noticed that there was something odd about his costume. Instead of roughout cowboy boots, he was sporting a pair of those weird, lace-up-the-side space boots. I decided I would go over and introduce myself.

Now, James Arness was a big man. He was so big that unless there was a point of reference, you couldn't estimate how big he really was. As I approached him, he seemed to grow. It was like hiking up to a giant redwood tree in the Sequoia National Forest. The closer I got, the bigger he became. If you recall the show, Matt's deputy, Chester, was a smallish-looking man played by Dennis Weaver. Using Dennis as a point of reference, it is important to note that Dennis was six foot two. I stuck out my hand and introduced myself.

"Mr. Arness, I'm Jim Hampton. I'm going to be playing Jeb this week."

"Well, I'm glad to meet you, son. I've heard a lot about you."

My entire hand and part of my forearm disappeared inside his as he pumped it enthusiastically.

"We don't stand on ceremony around here. Everybody calls me Jim."

A warmer welcome I couldn't imagine. I appreciated his little white lie about "hearing about me." There was nothing to hear about.

The entire cast was kind, friendly, and supportive. Between camera shots, we all sat in a circle of canvas set chairs with the cast's names on the back. Dennis Weaver, Amanda Blake, Milburn "Millie" Stone, Burt Reynolds, and the director all had one. My chair identified me as "Guest Star." To me, that was a huge deal. Mainly we shot the breeze or told jokes. Because we were always on hand and not off somewhere in an air-conditioned mobile home on a cell phone talking, texting, or tweeting, the shooting went swiftly, and the hour-long scripts were shot in five to seven days.

We rehearsed the scenes together, and sometimes, if the scripted scene seemed a little flat, Millie would get out a pencil and we would offer suggestions for changes. Often the scene would take on new life. It was that kind of dedication and spirit of cooperation that helped make *Gunsmoke* so popular for more than twenty years. I did three episodes of the show, and I was always treated as a member of the family. It had a great influence on me for the remainder of my career.

It was during the filming of my second *Gunsmoke* that the story I'm about to relate occurred. I was playing the part of Jeb once more, and plans were afoot to make Jeb a regular part of the cast. A new character was introduced that would provide a love interest for Jeb, played by the lovely, talented actress, Mariana Hill. The story was that I lived with my widower father, and Mariana's character had recently become an orphan. My father invited Mariana to live with us, and she would cook and clean in return for room and board. A family of vagabonds was passing through, and because of their greed for our tidy little ranch, my father was murdered. There was a scene at my father's grave where Matt Dillon paid his respects alongside two young people with uncertain futures. Mariana and I had no lines, and Jim carried the scene.

Pretty Lynn Loring and me in the *Gunsmoke* episode "Pa Hack's Brood." *Author Collection.*

We were filming in Thousand Oaks, California, on a ranch that was owned by the studio. It had gentle rolling hills and, at that time, showed no evidence of the twentieth century. Jim was napping in his modest little trailer (the same size as the rest of the cast), and the director, Jerry Hopper, was explaining the scene to Mariana, the director of photography, and me.

"We're going to do something a little different here. What I'm going for is a shot that emphasizes the loneliness of the situation. Three tiny specks around a little mound of earth with a simple wooden cross on the bleak Kansas horizon. I think it will heighten the sadness of the scene."

The director of photography began to nod enthusiastically.

"Both of you are now orphaned and completely alone. Mr. Arness is the only one with dialogue, so we're going to hook him up with a wireless mike. The camera will be down there about a hundred yards or so and with a wide-angle lens the sense of aloneness will be unbearable. Any questions?"

"Would you like me to cry?" Mariana asked.

Jerry shrugged. "I don't give a damn. Cry if you want to."

I thought, *Had she missed the tiny specks part?*

Jerry and the director of photography headed down to the camera location, I went back to my card game with the extras, and Mariana went off to gather wildflowers. It is my understanding that Mariana carried a notebook that helped her prepare for scenes. In it were reminders such as the death of a pet, the breakup of a love affair and the like, which served as emotional triggers to help her actually relive those moments during filming. Everyone has something in their bag of tricks. I once heard that when Bette Davis needed to make those luminous eyes tear up, she pulled out nose hair.

Just so there is no misunderstanding here, I want to tell you a little bit about Jim Arness. He and his brother Peter Graves (Arness is the family name) were born and educated in Minneapolis. I don't know if you have ever known anyone from Minnesota of Swedish or Norwegian descent, but if you have, you know they are hard-working, no-nonsense people. Jim had been in *The Farmer's Daughter* with Loretta Young, as well as several Westerns, including some with his friend John Wayne. Originally, Wayne was offered the part of Matt Dillon, but when he turned it down he recommended Jim for the role. It was the longest running drama (twenty seasons) in the history of television until *The Simpsons.*

Jim loved to surf and spent much of his spare time riding the waves in and around Malibu. Perhaps because of his upbringing, he was able to keep things in perspective. Jim won a Purple Heart at Anzio, so you know he wasn't afraid to fight for what he believed was right. After several years of playing Matt Dillon, it was rumored that he was able to get a clause in his contract that stipulated no filming past 6:00 p.m. There is purported to be a piece of film that shows Jim, walking out of a scene at six on the button. Despite entreaties from the director, Jim, without turning around, shoots the bird over his shoulder while disappearing through the exit.

This is my kind of guy. How many actors do you know who starred in their own series for two decades that have never had a bad word said about them? The answer is: one.

Jim did dislike a few things: overtime, regular cowboy boots, and tedious dialogue. After a few years, Jim could glance at a scene and boil a half page of dialogue down to, "Some of you men get this man up to Doc's office." Who could argue? Jim was Matt Dillon, and Matt was a man of few words.

Cowboy boots hurt his feet. I have no idea if his war injury had anything to do with that, but I do know that he hated to get on a horse because it meant he had to put on the odious boots. Everything else could be shot from knees up. That explains the space boots he was wearing on my first day on the set.

When Jim got bored waiting for scenes to be set, he would sometimes take a nap. The only one who was allowed to wake him up was his stand-in, Tiny. At six-foot-five, Tiny was slightly shorter than Jim, but weighed over three hundred pounds. He also had a heart as big as his frame and, over the years, rose from stand-in status to first assistant director. Tiny also had a pronounced stutter that asserted itself at the most inappropriate times and often diffused tense situations by causing everyone to laugh, including himself.

Once, a new director who didn't know that Jim always arrived exactly on time, but never late or early, was trying to set a precedent. Obviously, he had worked with stars that started late and caused production problems.

"You tell your boss if he isn't out here in exactly five minutes, he'll have to get a new director."

Tiny, who was already on his way to get Jim, stopped, slowly turned around and said, "W-w-well f-f-f-f … f-f-f-f … f-f-farewell then!"

Jim used to say that Tiny was worth his weight in gold, and that would have been quite a fortune. Tiny would have taken a bullet for Jim.

The news came that all was in readiness for the shot. Tiny was dispatched to rouse Jim and fetch Mariana and me so that we were waiting at the grave site when Jim arrived. Mariana had quite a bundle of wildflowers, and while she didn't want to break her concentration by making eye contact, I could tell she was really worked up over something she'd read in her notebook, probably that puppy-being-run-over-thing.

On the way from Jim's trailer, Tiny had briefed him on what the scene was, and had handed him the script page with the appropriate dialogue. Jim had given it a cursory glance and wadded up the page and tossed it aside.

He began to greet us when the soundman started wiring him up for the scene, to which Jim responded, "What are you doing there Glenn? Where the hell is everybody?"

I motioned towards the crew, a block away. The soundman explained what was going on.

"Cripes sake! What are we doing here, Red River?"

The soundman scurried away and the director's voice came over the electric megaphone.

"Jim, we are only going to do this once. There won't

be any coverage. If you need a rehearsal, just say so, but we are ready here."

Jim started to shout back that he was ready to go, but I pointed to his hidden mike inside his vest. Jim nodded.

"Jim to director, Jim to director. Message received loud and clear, Roger dodger, over and out."

Jim winked at me. He was having fun. Everything hushed as film prepared to roll.

We could hear the familiar commands, "Roll camera … Speed … and Action!"

As soon as action was given, Mariana knelt beside the grave and tenderly placed the wild flowers on the dirt mound. She began to sob. She was really heartbroken. Tiny hadn't mentioned flowers.

Jim looked at me in dismay as if to say, "Jim, what in the world have you said to this girl?"

I tried to indicate as subtly as possible with my eyes that none of this was my doing. Then, as the tears were forming rivulets and Mariana's nose began to run, Jim's eyes glazed over. It was the actor's nightmare. Whatever lines he had glanced at just minutes before had been permanently erased by a river of tears. Nevertheless, he knew that he had to say something. He removed his hat and held it over his heart. I waited breathlessly. Jim spoke.

"The Lord giveth, and the Lord taketh away. I'll kiss your ass if that ain't a square deal."

I wasn't sure I had heard him right. He put his hat back on, and I could see there was pandemonium down where the crew was. I started laughing and felt my knees giving away. Just before I toppled over, I saw that the tears in Mariana's eyes had been replaced by raw shock and hatred. Thank God it wasn't directed at me. There was no retrieving this one. The scene was cut. If you ever see the rerun called "Pa Hack's Brood," you'll never miss it.

My apologies to Miss Hill, but it was as funny a moment as I have ever witnessed.

JAMES GARNER

My pal Don Henley worked for Pat Boone, who had a contract over at Fox. Over lunch one day in the studio commissary, Don suggested we sneak onto the set of *The Thrill of It All* to see if we could get a peek at the stars, James Garner and Doris Day. Ms. Day was not on the set at the time, but Mr. Garner did not disappoint. From fifty feet away he radiated masculine charm. I thought Jim was just about the most handsome man I ever saw. He was the definition of a male movie star. I had seen the hugely successful comedies that Doris had made with Rock Hudson, of course, and I imagined that Mr. Garner had one of the most glamorous jobs on the planet. To think he actually got a paycheck for kissing Doris Day!

Much of the information I have on Jim I heard from one of the best friends I had in Hollywood, his brother Jack. You have undoubtedly seen Jack in many of Jim's movies and TV shows. Their family name is Bumgardner. There were three boys, as I recall, and all of them were outstanding athletes at their Norman, Oklahoma high school. Jack lettered four years in four sports and played baseball and golf professionally. Jim was the baby, and an equally gifted athlete and scratch golfer who could have easily been a professional as well. Before he graduated high school, Jim enlisted in the Coast Guard.

One of my favorite guys, James Garner on *The Rockford Files*. *Author Collection.*

After his distinguished and heroic service in Korea—Jim was modest about his medals, so I won't list them—the Bumgardners moved to California. Their father was in the carpet-laying business, and Jack and Jim laid carpet for their dad. It wasn't long before Jim's good looks and easygoing personality landed him a contract at Warner Brothers, and he was cast as Brett Maverick. He also starred in many feature films, and America loved him as Jim Rockford.

One of the great things about Jim was that when you met him, you felt as if you already knew him. The fact was, you did. Jim is exactly what he appears to be offscreen and onscreen. Whether it is *Murphy's Romance, Support Your Local Sheriff,* or *The Great Escape* (to name a very few), Jim's magnetic personality shines through. You could tell he was a genuinely nice guy. What you may not know is that, not surprisingly, he was generous as an actor and as a human being. When you were on a Jim Garner set, you felt none of the tension you sometimes experience on other sets. But he was no pushover. If he felt he was being cheated, he would go to the mat. He took on more than one studio when he felt he wasn't getting a square deal, and in every case he either won the court battle or gained financially by agreeing to a settlement. In other words, he was the perfect movie hero. He was charming, intelligent, friendly, straightforward, willing to stand up and fight when it was necessary, and in the end he always got the girl.

I was cast in the role of Aaron Ironwood on *Rockford Files* in an episode titled "Aaron Ironwood's School of Success." The show was extremely popular at the time, and this was a two-parter to kick off the season. Aaron Ironwood was one of my favorite roles, and people still ask me about it. Aaron was a charismatic con-man who was Rockford's adopted brother. Noah Beery (his friends called him Pidge), who played Jim's father, was continually separating the two brothers from punching each other's lights out.

We did have a fight scene though, and Jim wanted it to be as realistic as possible, but also amusing. In talking it over, we both remembered that when you fight your brother, even though you are mad enough to rip his head off, you had to obey certain unspoken rules. No biting, no eye-gouging, no kicking . . . well, maybe a little kicking from the younger brother—and when one brother gave up, the fight was over. We also remembered something else. You remove your ring, if you have one, because it could cut your brother's face, and you take off your watch because you don't want it to get broken.

Probably no one would know what we were doing, but Jim was nice enough to sell the idea to the director. I was wearing a solid gold Pulsar watch that Burt Reynolds had given me after *The Longest Yard*. It was the flashiest piece of jewelry that I had, and a perfect accessory for Aaron. Just before the fight between Jim and I began, I halted the procedures, took off my watch, carefully placed it aside and sucker punched him. I'll never forget Jim's line, which he delivered in complete astonishment.

"Ow! Now that hurt!"

After the show aired, a kid about twelve years old came up to me after church.

Kid: "I saw you on *The Rockford Files*. You took off your watch before the fight. I liked that!"

Me: "Do you have an older brother?"

Kid: "Sure do!"

Me: "You guys ever get into fights?"

Kid: "Yeah, sometimes."

Me: "You ever win?"

The kid shook his head.

Me: "Try kicking him next time."

I never felt better leaving church.

JANE FONDA

I met Jane Fonda as a result of being cast in the role of Bill Gibson in *The China Syndrome*. I was thrilled to be in company that included Jack Lemmon, Michael Douglas, Scott Brady, Wilford Brimley, and on and on. When I first read the script, written by T. S. Cook and directed by Jim Bridges, my excitement waned somewhat. At a time when movies with a catastrophe plot were in vogue, this one didn't exactly fit the mold. There was no catastrophe! No burning skyscraper. No earthquake. No upside-down sinking ship.

Someone asked me what the movie was about, and I said, "Something almost happens in the first twenty minutes, we talk about it for the next hour, then something almost happens in the last twenty minutes."

I thought I was being clever. Actually, I was being pretty stupid. Jane, Jack, and Michael (who also produced the movie) thought enough of the script to perform for scale, which was absolutely unheard of at the time. As children, we were told we would be judged by the company we keep. In the case of this cast, I was in pretty rarified company.

The first scene I did was the very beginning of the film, when a film crew comes to a nuclear power plant to do a soft piece for a TV news show. My character was to welcome them and show them around. When I formed the scene in my mind, I felt that my character, the public relations representative for the power plant, would be awkwardly thrilled to be around Kimberly Wells (Jane Fonda), a TV celebrity. This took absolutely no acting on my part as it was exactly how I felt.

Later we were rehearsing a scene in an elevator at the power plant. After the second run-through, Jane said to me, "I don't think Mr. Gibson would say that line, do you?"

I was caught completely off guard. Before I was able to stop myself, I answered, "Yes, I do, and I'll tell you why."

And I did. When I turned to her, she was smiling

Fantastic cast of *The China Syndrome*. *Author Collection.*

quizzically. From some of the things I had heard about Jane, not to mention the pillorying she got for her opposition to the Vietnam War, the last thing I would have imagined was a quizzical smile for a difference of opinions.

Filming another scene later during the making of the movie, we went on location in Chatsworth, California, a few miles north of the San Fernando Valley. As we were loading up the cast in station wagons, Jane called out to me, "Jim, get in here and ride with us."

With that, she scooted over toward the teamster who was assigned to drive her, and I got in up front. The rest of the car was full of hair and makeup people.

"Tell us some jokes, Jim," she said.

So, I told jokes for the next half hour or so, and no one laughed louder or clapped their hands harder than Jane did. When we arrived on location, as I helped her out of the car, she very quietly said to me, "I'm not like what they told you, am I?"

All I could do was shake my head. She had read my mind.

That year Jane was up for an Oscar for her role in *Julia,* along with Vanessa Redgrave, who won. The morning after the Academy Awards, we were shooting in the power plant. I was sitting in the makeup chair and saw Jane come in slightly late and a bit haggard. The entire room froze in their tracks and all activity stopped. Nobody knew what to do or say. Jane looked embarrassed and vulnerable. I knew how she must have felt.

I shouted out, "Hey Jane! I fell asleep last night. Did you win anything?"

There was a silent second or two, and at least as many gasps until Jane broke the silence. She threw back her head and laughed. And in doing so, she gave us permission to join her. But Jane laughed the hardest. Great, healing, rollicking laughter. She winked and gave me that private look that she did when I helped her out of the car on location.

No Jane, you weren't like what they told me.

China Syndrome Chop Suey

INGREDIENTS

3-4 cups of steak, cut into ⅓" cubes

Salt and pepper to taste

Bacon drippings

4 cups celery, cut into ½" lengths

1 cup diced onion

1 can of bean sprouts

½ cup tomato juice

1 small can of mushrooms

1 tablespoon molasses

4-6 tablespoons soy sauce

3-4 tablespoons of cornstarch

1 can crunchy lo mein noodles

DIRECTIONS

Brown meat and season with salt and pepper to taste. Set aside. Brown celery and onion in bacon drippings and put into a large kettle, big enough for all ingredients. Drain can of bean sprouts over the celery and onion, adding just enough water to cover. Cook until tender. Add tomato juice, bean sprouts, mushrooms, meat, and molasses, and cook for 10 minutes.

(NOTE: If the meat is not tender and completely cooked after browning, allow it to cook a bit longer with the celery and onion.)

Make a thin paste with cornstarch and soy sauce and add to the kettle. Stir over heat until thickened. Serve hot with rice and lo mein noodles.

JIMMY STEWART

In the early 70s, I was chosen to play one of Jimmy Stewart's nephews on his television series, *Hawkins On Murder* (Mayf Nutter played the other nephew). The nephews would assist their uncle in investigating cases, while infusing some youth into the story lines. It was one of those rare occasions when I was picked by the producer without an audition. The money was generous, and all I needed to do before I began shooting the following week was to have an informal meeting with the director. Things were done with much less fuss in those days.

The show was being filmed at MGM, and my appointment was at the director's office on the lot. I have never driven through that studio gate, guarded by concrete lions, without feeling the excitement of being on holy ground. Metro Goldwyn Mayer (now Sony) was the epitome of all things Hollywood, including the ironic fact that it was actually in Culver City. In its heyday, it had the biggest stars under contract, the biggest movies being produced (*Gone With The Wind*, *The Wizard of Oz*), and it even had the biggest soundstages. One stage could be flooded and naval battles waged there. It was the Yankee Stadium of studios. Now there I was, about to "take a meeting" at MGM for a show starring Jimmy Stewart!

I mounted the steps of the Producer's Building to meet with the director, Jud Taylor. After congratulating me and offering me coffee, Jud asked if I had ever worked with Mr.

With Jimmy Stewart in *Hawkins on Murder*. Author Collection.

Stewart before. I told him I had no recollection of working with him and I was pretty sure I would have remembered if I had. Thank goodness Jud had a sense of humor and it broke the ice, so we could get down to business. The purpose of the meeting was to give me a couple of tips about working with Mr. Stewart.

Tip Number One: Try not to get into Mr. Stewart's rhythm. Mr. Stewart had a style all his own, and if you weren't careful, when you did a scene with him, you could pick up his cadence. Before you knew it, you would be sounding like somebody doing a bad impression of Jimmy Stewart.

Jud assured me, "Don't worry too much about it. It happens to everybody."

Tip Number Two: Try not to pause too long. Mr. Stewart had a little hearing loss, but he didn't want to wear a hearing aid while filming. He watched the other actor's mouth, and when it stopped moving, he would say his next line. So, I needed to watch my pauses and stay away from his rhythm. I could do that.

I thanked Jud for his tips, told him I looked forward to working with him, and left. During the course of filming the next two or three shows, I did both of the things Jud warned me against. It was impossible not to.

On the drive back to Encino, I remembered a story I had been told about Jimmy Stewart early on in my career. I was at a party that Brenda Vacarro and Jessica Walter had thrown and found myself talking to George Peppard. I was not used to Hollywood parties, and I certainly didn't expect to meet such a huge movie star. I was a big fan of George Peppard and was totally taken aback. I had actually modeled myself after him. I liked his style of understated acting. I even had the same haircut, but I was almost dumbstruck at meeting him so unexpectedly. I didn't know what to say. He laughed, said he understood, and told me a story that put me completely at ease.

After the success of *Breakfast at Tiffany's* with Audrey Hepburn, George was an instant star. He was cast as the lead in *How The West Was Won*. Jimmy Stewart was just one of the mega-stars in that movie. Stewart had always been George's favorite actor, and as the day approached when he would be working with him, George grew more and more nervous. He felt like an upstart. He thought Jimmy Stewart should play the lead, not he! The night before he was to work with Mr. Stewart, George couldn't sleep. What do you say to Mount Rushmore? How do you act?

Do you say something like, "Gee, Mr. Stewart, I can't believe you're here." Or, "I've been looking forward to meeting you Mr. Stewart. I'm a big fan of yours." No, he wanted to be professional about it. What about something simple and honest?

George settled on: "How do you do Mr. Stewart? I'm George Peppard. I certainly have enjoyed your work."

That was it. He rehearsed the line several times. "How do you do Mr. Stewart? I'm George Peppard. I certainly have enjoyed your work."

Finally, he went to bed.

The next morning was an early call. The first thing George wanted when he arrived on the set was a cup of steaming black coffee to clear the cobwebs and get his day going. He had just poured himself a cup at the craft service wagon when he felt a tap on his shoulder. He turned around to see a cheerful man in buckskins and a coonskin cap.

"How do you do Mr. Peppard? I'm Jimmy Stewart. I certainly have enjoyed your work."

I have always loved that story because it not only

Practicing my George Peppard look. *Author Collection.*

shows what a gracious man Jimmy Stewart was, it also shows what a down-to-earth guy George was.

My first meeting with Mr. Stewart was not as auspicious. I met him in the makeup room. I was in the chair getting powdered down when he came in. He had a floppy little golf hat on. He never appeared without his hat until he had his toupee in place.

"Is that my new nephew over there?" he inquired and I leaped to my feet.

"Yes, Sir, Mr. Stewart."

"Call me Jimmy, son. Mr. Stewart was my old man."

At that moment I knew how George Peppard felt. Jimmy was completely genuine. He made all the butterflies in my stomach fly away. He was that way with everyone. I saw him cross only once. He was astounded and disappointed at a well-known guest star's lack of preparation. The actor was amused when he blew his lines repeatedly. Jimmy Stewart was not.

The first scene we had together was on location in Newhall. It was on a deserted stretch of road that is now a main thoroughfare for a thriving community. In the story, we were investigating a crime scene, looking for clues to exonerate a client that Hawkins was defending. We had a few lines, got in our car, and I drove us away. Cut, print, end of scene.

The sound department had put a walkie-talkie on the front seat of the car between Jimmy and me so we could be in touch with the assistant director. After we drove away, the assistant director would inform us when the scene was cut and whether or not it was a print. It was a simple enough scene, and we actors were doing our job well, but for some reason we had to repeat the scene a few times. There was no explanation, to me anyway, just orders to come on back and do it again.

After about four times, as we were driving away, sure enough, the assistant director came on the walkie-talkie to direct us back to the first position. I was about to make a U-turn when Jimmy spoke up.

Jimmy: "Just keep going."

Me: "Do what?"

Jimmy: "Just keep on driving. We're going to have a little fun."

The walkie-talkie crackled again.

"Come back to the first position, copy?"

I didn't answer the assistant director.

Me: "We're going to get in trouble."

Jimmy: "No, we won't."

We were disappearing over a hill beyond the sight of the crew. Jimmy reached over and turned off the walkie-talkie.

Jimmy: "I made a movie not too long ago with Hank Fonda, *The Cheyenne Social Club.* You ever see it?"

Me: "Sure. Ken Berry's wife, Jackie Joseph, was in it."

Jimmy: "That's right. Well, you know Hank and I have been pals a long time. We had to do a lot of riding in that movie for the opening sequence. So one day we'd just had enough. We rode over the hill and kept on going. We had the walkie-talkie in my saddlebag and they were just going crazy trying to get us. We rode all the way back to town and had lunch."

Me: "Did you get in trouble?"

Jimmy: "No, no, we told them the walkie-talkie was broken. Okay, I guess we've worried them enough. Let's turn around and head on back."

I made a U-turn and headed back. About a mile down the road, we met the assistant director who was frantically looking for us. Jimmy told him they needed to replace the battery in the walkie-talkie. The assistant director gave me a murderous look. I shrugged. What was the assistant director going to do, call Jimmy Stewart a liar? God that was fun!

I wish I had the eloquence to describe what it was like to work with Jimmy. He was an exemplary man and a total professional. We had the best crew in town, and that was because of him. Who wouldn't want to work with Jimmy Stewart? I was smoking in those days, and our director of photography, Dick Konnekamp, and his crew could light a scene before I could finish my cigarette. Everybody did their best to try to ease some of Jimmy's load, but he never asked for special treatment. As the star, he had tons of dialogue, much of it courtroom legal jargon. It must have been tough on him. Many times I saw him start to run out of gas in the late afternoon, but the moment he was called to the set, the years and the fatigue would fall away.

During our lunch breaks, while the rest of us went to the commissary, Jimmy would retire to his trailer. He always brought the lunch his wife had packed him in a black metal lunch box, just like any working stiff. He took his lunch break that way every day while he studied his lines for the afternoon scenes.

One day we had flown through the day's work. It was just past four in the afternoon, and we were two thirds of the way through the final scene.

The assistant director approached me and said, "Jim, we only have your close-up left. Would you mind if the script supervisor does Jimmy's off-camera dialogue with you? That way we can let Jimmy go home early."

I said, "Of course not, I don't mind at all."

The assistant director went over to Jimmy and told him he was free to go home. As Jimmy was about to sign the sign-out sheet, he looked over at me.

Then, he said, "Wait a second. What about Jim's close-up?"

The assistant director replied, "Dorothy's going to read your off-camera lines. I talked to Jim about it and he's fine with it. If you leave now you can beat the traffic."

I looked over at Jimmy and gave him the thumbs up sign. Jimmy rose out of his seat.

He said, "Oh no! This is all wrong. You can't do that to another actor. It wouldn't be the same. No offense to Dorothy, but it just wouldn't."

The assistant director could see he wasn't going to get anywhere, so he tried a new tactic and argued "Okay then, I can see your point, but we've got to put a wall in and do a total reverse on lighting. It's probably going to take half an hour. Why don't you go in your trailer, take off the toop, get out of your wardrobe, and relax? I'll come and get you when we're ready."

I never saw Jimmy get so worked up. It was straight out of *Mr. Smith Goes to Washington.* He was apoplectic.

"No, no, NO! Don't you get it? That's all wrong. Jim isn't doing a scene with Jimmy Stewart! He's doing a scene with his uncle. His uncle doesn't dress like me! He's got hair, for gosh sakes! No! I'm sorry. But you can't do that to another actor. That wouldn't be right! That just wouldn't be fair. No, no. I appreciate what you're doing here, but I can't do that. I'm sorry."

About forty-five minutes later, we finished the scene. There was applause at the end. It wasn't for me. Jimmy Stewart acted just as hard for me off-camera as he did in his own close-up. He matched everything he had done in the master so if the editor wanted to cut at any time to my reaction, it would match. If he stood up, my eyes would be in the right position; if he paced back and forth, my eyes would follow him.

Nowadays it is common practice to do close-ups with the script supervisor, but Jimmy was right. It does make a difference.

JIM NABORS

My friend George Lindsey went on to become Goober on *The Andy Griffith Show*, and he invited me over for lunch and to meet the cast and crew. I met Jim Nabors that day, and it wasn't long before he had his own very successful show called simply *Gomer Pyle, U.S.M.C.* He had told me even before the show began that he would find a part for me, which he did. I played the part of Branch Eversole on an episode called "The Feuding Pyles."

Jim had a sneaky sense of humor that kidnapped you before you saw it coming. Through the years, we would occasionally run into each other. Jim was a big star in Las Vegas and a regular guest on *The Carol Burnett Show*. His success allowed him to buy a huge macadamia nut plantation worth millions near Carol's property in Maui. The last time I saw him, he was coming out of the William Morris Agency and I was going in. This was our brief conversation:

Him: "Hey Jim! How are you?"

Me: "For goodness sake, Jim! I heard you moved to Maui. What is the world are you doing there?"

Him: "Oh, just waiting for my nuts to fall!"

A collage of photos from my episode of Gomer Pyle. *Author Collection.*

Jim Nabors's Hawaiian Pineapple Macadamia Nut Biscuits

INGREDIENTS

1 10-ounce can crushed pineapple
½ cup light brown sugar, packed
½ stick butter, softened
1 small package macadamia nuts
1 can buttermilk biscuits, 10 count

DIRECTIONS

Preheat oven to 400 degrees. Grease muffin tin. Drain pineapple and reserve juice. Mix together pineapple, sugar, and butter. Divide pineapple mixture at the bottom of each muffin cup (for 10 biscuits). Place a few macadamia nuts on top of pineapple mixture and add a biscuit to each. Pour 1 teaspoon of reserved pineapple juice on top of each biscuit. Bake for 12-15 minutes or until golden brown. Set aside to cool for 2 minutes. Invert muffin pan over plate to release the biscuits. Serve warm and say "Shazam!" after your first bite.

JOHNNY CARSON

I don't think I ever sat and watched *The Tonight Show* and imagined that someday I would be sitting across from the host trading clever dialogue. I got hooked on late-night television when a show called *Broadway Open House* starring Buddy Lester appeared. Buddy had honed his act in the Catskills and always wore a tuxedo and flirted outrageously with the not-so-dumb blonde, Dagmar. Buddy was short and Dagmar was tall, so when they had a conversation, Buddy was eye-to-eye, so to speak, with her ample bosom. It was straight out of burlesque and never failed to make me laugh. Over the years other hosts have sat behind the desk and not only have they entertained us, they have also become part of our family. There was Jack Paar, Steve Allen, and eventually Dick and Merv and Chevy and Dave and Jay and all the others, but there was never anyone who came close to Mr. Johnny Carson. Believe me. I know whereof I speak. Here's how it happened.

Burt Reynolds was the guest host of *The Tonight Show* the same night his centerfold appearance debuted in *Cosmopolitan Magazine*. He had asked me to come to Chicago, where he was doing a play, and fly with him to New York for moral support, and I agreed. This was before big stars traveled with a retinue of sycophants. Burt's guests that night included his ex-wife Judy Carne (of *Laugh-In* fame) with whom he had an amicable relationship at that time. I worked up a couple of jokes for him, and the show was huge. Later, he and I were on *The Merv Griffin Show*, *The Mike Douglas Show*, and, of course, Dinah's talk show, as we plugged *The Longest Yard*. All of them were quite

With the one and only Mr. Johnny Carson. *Courtesy of Carson Entertainment Group.*

good in their own way. I guess you have to have a knack for it.

After things had settled down, out of the blue I got a call from *The Tonight Show*. They wanted me for the following night!

I had a very fitful night's sleep and was awakened early by the sounds of sanitation men picking up the trash down the street. I pulled the pillow over my head to keep out the scraping, banging, screeching, mashing, clinking, clanging, and something that sounded like a tape of a lioness giving birth played backwards.

How inconsiderate, I thought. *Don't these people know I'm going to be on* The Tonight Show *in a few hours? I need my rest.*

I'm not kidding. I actually thought that.

111

Well, it was no use trying to get a few more hours sleep. I swung my legs off the bed and asked myself, *How does one prepare for* The Tonight Show? *There are no lines to learn. So what do I do? What is Johnny going to ask me? Should I tell a joke?*

Suddenly I couldn't remember one joke that I could tell on the air.

Okay, so that's out. We'll just talk. The two of us. Me and Johnny. Yeah, just me and Johnny and twenty or thirty million people. I stood up.

Yikes! If I knew I was going to be on The Tonight Show, *I would have lost a little weight. Getting a little paunch going there. Okay, I won't eat anything today. Oh sure, that will be a big help! What can I do? Okay, how about personal hygiene? I can do that. I can get really, really clean. Shampoo, conditioner, gargling, flossing, deodorant, and a generous application of Aramis! I may be a dud, and I may never be asked back, but at least they can say, "You know, that Hampton, he wasn't very funny, but man he sure smelled good."*

I filled a bath with hot sudsy water. I soaked, I scrubbed, I shaved, I shampooed, I conditioned, I toweled, I moisturized, I clipped, I re-shaved, brushed, and flossed. The whole process took about an hour. That left about eight hours before I was due at the Burbank Studios and plenty of time to obsess into a quivering mass of anxiety. Nobody will like me and two tall men in hats and dark overcoats will arrest me for intent to represent oneself as a celebrity. In Hollywood, you can get life for that.

By then, I was again peering at my now red and splotchy naked pudginess in the mirror, and bemoaning the fact I still didn't have a clue as to what I was going to say to America that night, when I remembered something I thought might come in handy. I heard somewhere that Van Johnson, who was doing dinner theater at the time, had, with age, developed a thicker middle. His solution was to wrap himself with Saran Wrap as a sort of invisible girdle. I thought that was just crazy enough to work.

I dashed to the kitchen. Eureka! There was a new roll of Saran Wrap. My plan was to make a test wrap and if it worked, fine, but if it didn't, I wouldn't have to explain or listen to a nutritional lecture about too much fried foods and ice cream. I was flushed with excitement at my cleverness. I remembered seeing a photo of the famous Helden tenor Lauritz Melchior being stuffed into a corset prior to a performance of "Die Dämmerung." Hey, whatever works.

I sucked my gut in as best I could and, standing naked in front of the mirror, I began to unroll the clear plastic stuff and wrap it around my midsection. After a couple of wraps I could see this was going to be a success. Then something odd happened. If you have ever tried to rip off a few inches of Saran Wrap to cover a casserole, you know that sometimes you have trouble getting it to tear where you want it to. Instead of twelve to fourteen inches, you end up with a yard and a half. To be successful you must rip it with a sharp downward motion. Try doing it sideways with a sharp upward motion. On second thought, don't try. Trust me, it can't be done. You would have to do what I did, which was to unroll the stuff until there was nothing left but the cardboard. It took some time, as it was a brand-new roll.

I was beginning to sweat a little, and while I was not exactly gasping for breath, I felt the burn. I evaluated myself in the mirror and concluded the plastic corset was working. I decided I needed to see what I looked like with clothes on. I grabbed a pair of black socks and sat on the edge of the bed, but when I leaned over to put one on, the Saran Wrap rolled up or more accurately, down. It looked less like a sash and more like a garden hose. This was a problem. I rolled it back up and hopped around on one foot to get my socks on. I could roll it back up, but if I sat down, it rolled down again under my belly like Levi's on the Michelin Man. Obviously this wasn't working out. It would seem odd if I did *The Tonight Show* standing up. I stood up, rolled the wrap back up, and began to look for the end so I could unwind fifty yards of Saran Wrap.

Anyone who has ever used cellophane tape to wrap a present or seal an envelope knows how frustrating it is when you can't find the end of the tape. Multiply that frustration by a thousand to approach what I was feeling. And let me say, Saran Wrap is tough stuff. You could tow a boat with it. You could make a pool cover out of that stuff. You can't tear it; you can't rip it. I dare you to try if you know where the end is. I did the only thing I know how to do in this sort of situation. I panicked. Perspiration was charting a course down my butt crack like the Colorado River through the Grand Canyon. I began to claw at the cellophane. I was able to tear off some insignificant shreds of the stuff, but it wasn't budging. I was going to need a chainsaw. I admit I wasn't thinking clearly. I looked up to see my reflection. It was of a sweaty, wild-eyed, deranged, naked man (except for black socks, which is really worse), with slivers of plastic hanging from his fingernails, breathless and beaten.

While this would have been a good story, that night Johnny and I ended up talking about my vasectomy. Even better.

I appeared on *The Tonight Show* more than thirty times and with several guest hosts including Burt, Bob Newhart, Bill Cosby, and Fernando Lamas. But before I ever appeared on *The Tonight Show*, I watched it like millions of others, and I discovered a secret that was valuable later on. Lots of comedians got a shot on the show, but they never made it to the couch. The ones that made it to the couch didn't always make it back. It is also true that many actors, authors, and other important people didn't make the couch more than once. Here's the secret: Never play to the audience. If Johnny laughs, so will they.

When a new comic would come on and do five or six minutes of the best material they had, during the subsequent response from the audience Johnny would either invite him or her over to the couch or not. What happened next was crucial. During the next few minutes, whatever the comic did or said had to be to Johnny, not to the audience. The same went for everybody. If someone was there to plug a book or a movie, they had to relate to Johnny. The audience, whether at home or in the studio, were like flies on the wall. They were there to respond to but not take part in two people having a conversation. Johnny would become the straight man and set up the jokes, but the punch line had to break Johnny up. If it worked, the person went on to fame and fortune and his own TV show,

but if it didn't work, well, neither did that person.

I was probably the only person in the history of *The Tonight Show* who did the show for the money. I thought that getting four hundred bucks for talking to Johnny Carson for seven or eight minutes was a pretty good gig. Also, I didn't mind being on last. Most people wanted to get on as early as possible to have the largest audience. In my case, I wasn't usually plugging anything and, as I said, I did it to help pay the bills. Plus, the show had a wonderful policy: If you were booked but time ran out before your spot, Johnny would apologize, and you were invited back the next night. So you got two intros, two apologies, and—best of all—two checks! Sounds like a deal to me.

A lot of things have been said about Johnny over the years, both pro and con. I am happy to report he was always nice to me and unfailingly funny. He was kind, thoughtful, and well mannered. While there was always a pre-interview, and notes to Johnny pointing him in a direction for the guest to respond, he didn't always do that. In my case, he almost never referred to the notes. He liked to wing it. He liked spontaneity. You almost never saw Johnny before the show. He didn't want to "leave the show backstage." Nevertheless, I was surprised one night to see Johnny in the makeup mirror smiling at me.

He had an idea for the show that night and he wanted to check with me to see if I was on board. Johnny said that he and his wife were lying in bed the night before and some movie or TV rerun that I was in came on the screen. He asked Joanne if she knew my name. She admitted that she had seen me countless times, but for some reason she couldn't remember my name. This gave birth to his idea. He wanted to know how I felt about not billboarding my name at the beginning of the show and going on with no introduction. Then he would poll the studio audience: Did they recognize me? And did they know my name?

The producers thought it was a little chancy, because if they didn't recognize me, the joke died. Johnny made it clear that if doing this made me uncomfortable in any way, he would scrap the whole idea and stick to the script. I told him I thought it was hilarious. People often approached me who not only couldn't remember my name, they often wanted me to tell them what they had seen me in!

The gag went off well. In his intros, Ed teased the audience by referring to me as "a mystery guest." Johnny set it up brilliantly. He told the story of Joanne's inability to recall my name. He read off a list of my movie and TV credits, and then they brought me out. I think Doc Severinsen and *The Tonight Show* band played the *F Troop* theme. After the applause died down, Johnny asked the studio audience to applaud if they had ever seen me before. Everyone clapped. Then he asked if anyone knew my name. Nobody clapped. Not one person. So where do you go from there? Johnny knew. He made everyone put their hand over their heart and pledge "to remember the name of James Hampton."

That was many years ago. To this day, sometimes someone will come up to me and say, "You're James Hampton aren't you?" I always respond, "You took the pledge didn't you?" A few years ago, at one of my wife's sorority functions, I met a fellow, Ken DePriest, who was actually in the live audience that day. He was a college student at the time, in town from Oregon with his fraternity on a school break. Small world, huh?

Before our move to Texas, my wife, Mary, and her dear friend Helen Sanders, Johnny's lovely and stalwart assistant for more than two decades, arranged a lunch with Johnny near his office in Santa Monica. Johnny's nephew, Jeff, joined us. One of *The Tonight Show*'s writers, Bob Smith, was also there. The three of us told jokes nonstop. I noticed Johnny directed a lot of his jokes to Mary. Smitten by his charm, she hung on every word. He always knew where his audience was. It was the last time I ever saw him.

One of my favorite remembrances of him isn't when I killed on the show but one night when I tanked. *The Tonight Show* had flown me to New York where they were taping. I told a story about getting lost on the subway years before. The story died; so did I. Have you ever wondered what Johnny was saying to his guests when he leaned over to them seconds before the commercial break? That night, Johnny leaned over to me and whispered, "You ought to call that story subway to the shit house!" We both laughed like idiots. There will never be anyone else like Mr. Johnny Carson. I miss you, pal. We all do.

Always the guy next door. Headshot from the '80s. *Author Collection.*

(Top) Loved spending time with Johnny Carson. (Bottom) I had lots of laughs with Johnny Carson. *Courtesy of Carson Entertainment Group.*

Heeeeeeere's Johnny's Black-eyed Pea Relish

I brought some black-eyed peas to Johnny Carson one New Year's Eve when I was a guest on the show!

INGREDIENTS

½ pound black-eyed peas

1 teaspoon sugar

2 tablespoons bacon fat

2 cups chopped dill pickles

1 cup chopped green pepper (small dice)

1 cup chopped red onion (small dice)

¼ cup each of chopped red and yellow pepper (small dice)

¼ teaspoon garlic powder

½ cup chopped green onions

2 tablespoons chopped garlic

Dash of hot sauce

1 seeded and finely chopped jalapeño pepper

Salt and pepper to taste

DIRECTIONS

Rinse black-eyed peas in cold water, removing any rocks. (Yes, rocks. There are always a few little ones in the bag, don't ask me why.) Cover in cold water and soak overnight. They will soften. Drain and rinse. Cover the black-eyed peas in fresh water, adding sugar and bacon fat. Bring to a boil. Do NOT overcook. Peas should be firm, not mushy. Drain. Place the black-eyed peas in large bowl, adding the remaining ingredients, and refrigerate until ready to eat. Serve the relish with your favorite tortilla chips. Muy Bueno!

JOHNNY CASH

Working with The Man in Black, Johnny Cash. *Author Collection.*

Caretaker is Manager on *The Longest Yard. Author Collection.*

When my agent told me I'd be working on a film starring Johnny Cash, it caught me off guard. I'd always thought of The Man in Black as a singer, not an actor, but lots of entertainers have made that crossover. In any event, I was anxious to meet him. I figured we had a lot in common. After all, hadn't I auditioned for the Texas Boys Choir as a kid?

The picture was *Thaddeus Rose and Eddie* and also starred Diane Ladd and Bo Hopkins. I played a shifty real estate agent with a catchy commercial jingle. "Alvin Karl, he sells Texas, Alvin Karl he sells Texas . . . " I do indeed sell Johnny's character a derelict grapefruit orchard in South Texas, which comes with its own resident picker.

Johnny had a great sense of humor. I guess you'd have to after spending a lot of time in prisons. Contrary to popular belief, he never served more than a day but enjoyed performing concerts in many prisons, entertaining the internees for whom he had much compassion.

I had spent a few months at the Georgia State Prison in Reidsville shooting *The Longest Yard.* Every morning our cast and crew would be locked down inside the gates with some of the most dangerous criminals in Georgia to film the scenes for the day. In fact, most of the extras in the movie were actual prisoners. Not a big stretch acting-wise, but the guys were eager to participate, and it was a welcome distraction. Personally, I always thought those prison cheerleaders in the film were marvelous.

After *The Longest Yard* was released, Burt and I did a television special at a maximum-security prison in the middle of nowhere. There were about five hundred inmates in a cafeteria-turned-auditorium anxiously awaiting anything remotely resembling entertainment. While they were setting up, a camera lens broke and another had to be brought in from the nearest big city before filming could begin.

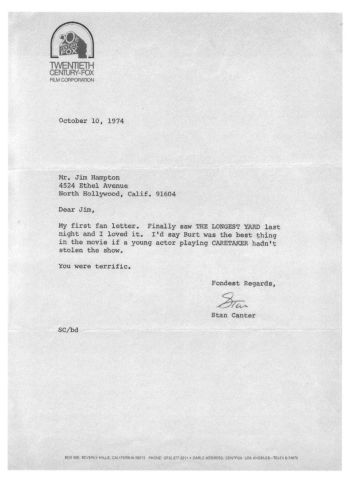

Fan letter from Stan Canter. *Author Collection.*

TWENTIETH CENTURY-FOX FILM CORPORATION

October 10, 1974

Mr. Jim Hampton
4524 Ethel Avenue
North Hollywood, Calif. 91604

Dear Jim,

My first fan letter. Finally saw THE LONGEST YARD last night and I loved it. I'd say Burt was the best thing in the movie if a young actor playing CARETAKER hadn't stolen the show.

You were terrific.

Fondest Regards,

Stan Canter

SC/bd

BOX 900, BEVERLY HILLS, CALIFORNIA 90213 PHONE: (213) 277-2211 • CABLE ADDRESS: CENTFOX, LOS ANGELES—TELEX 6-74675

Meanwhile, Yours Truly was asked by the producers to keep everyone amused for about an hour. Lucky for me, I had a captive audience—literally.

The "hour" turned into three, and despite my compelling charms I was starting to smell a riot brewing. Burt and the rest of my costars had vamoosed and were probably downing flat sodas and stale pretzels in a makeshift green room somewhere. The producers, meanwhile, were continuing to motion to me with wild eyes and flailing arms to keep things going. Just then I devised a brilliant plan. Nothing like a rousing round of "Row, Row, Row Your Boat," right? As if conducting the Mormon Tabernacle Choir, I lifted my invisible baton and began, "Okay! Let's start off with the arsonists . . . Row, row, row your boat . . . " They complied, and I felt like Antal Doráti. "Now the armed robbers . . . Row, row, row your boat . . . " The second group launched into song and I was Glenn Miller. "Great! Now the drug traffickers . . . Row, row, row your boat . . . " There was no riot, tear gas, or mayhem. Suddenly, everyone was having a fantastic time. Yes, the Nursery Rhyme Gods were with me that day.

A day's shooting on *Thaddeus Rose and Eddie* typically wound down after dinner with Johnny, his wife, June Carter Cash, their posse, and some of the members of our cast just hanging out and making music. The gospel songs were the best. Singing along with them, even I sounded like an angel.

Johnny Cash-ew in a Wok

INGREDIENTS

1 bunch broccoli
½ pound round steak
2 tablespoons oyster sauce
½ teaspoon salt
1 to 2 teaspoons sugar, or to taste
¼ cup chicken broth
1 teaspoon cornstarch
1 teaspoon soy sauce
2 tablespoons water
2 tablespoons peanut or vegetable oil
1 8-ounce can water chestnuts
2 cups cashews

DIRECTIONS

Break broccoli tops into small florets. Use tops only; trim off rough ends. Cut into ½" slices and boil for 3 minutes. Drain and set aside. Slice round steak into thin pieces against the grain. In a small bowl, combine oyster sauce, salt, sugar, and broth. In another bowl, blend cornstarch, soy sauce, and water into a paste. Heat oil in a wok, add beef and stir-fry about 2 minutes or until beef loses its redness. Add broccoli and water chestnuts. Stir in oyster sauce mix and heat quickly. Stir in cornstarch paste to thicken slightly, then add cashews. Must be served at once. Yield: Dinner for two and great over rice!

BERNADETTE PETERS

Burt Reynolds knew how to throw a party. Not long after we wrapped shooting *The Longest Yard* in Georgia, he had a little shindig for some friends whom he had missed while we were away filming.

While I enjoyed playing the wonderful role of Caregiver in the movie, my one regret was that I never had the chance to meet our costar, the beautiful Bernadette Peters. We had no scenes together. We were never even on the set on the same days. So when Burt told me she had been invited to his party, I was keen to go. I had the tiniest crush on Miss Peters.

I showered. I shaved. I trimmed my nose hairs.

Bernadette was indeed at the party but was oblivious that I was in attendance. Or, in fact, that I even existed. I watched from afar, looking for an opportunity to say hello, but the evening dragged on without one. Discouraged, I plopped down on one of the chic, uncomfortable cushions scattered on the living room floor of Burt's perfect 70s bachelor pad and focused on eating hors d'oeuvres. I soon forgot about my quest to meet Bernadette.

It got late, the party was thinning out, and I was still sitting cross-legged on the floor. Only now, I couldn't feel anything below my waist. Word to the wise: Do not sit cross-legged on the floor after the age of thirty. Charles Nelson Reilly, in his delightful, flamboyant style, was regaling us with some witty stories when I suddenly felt a pair of hands rubbing my neck and shoulders. I scanned the room. I didn't see Bernadette. I found myself entertaining the notion that *she* was behind me, massaging my levator scapulae.

I quickly concocted a plan that involved me saying something incredibly charming and clever. Almost shaking with anticipation, I turned around.

It wasn't Bernadette.

It was Dom DeLuise.

You can only imagine my disappointment.

Bernadette Biscuits with Chocolate Gravy

INGREDIENTS FOR BISCUITS

½ cup (1 stick) plus 2 tablespoons cold unsalted butter or lard (Note: Lard makes the biscuits fluffier)
Additional butter or lard to grease baking sheet
2 ¼ cups self-rising soft wheat flour (Note: If you can get it, use White Lily)
Pinch of salt
1 ½ cups well-shaken buttermilk
2 tablespoons cold unsalted butter for the pan
Additional flour for kneading

DIRECTIONS

Preheat oven to 425 degrees. Lightly butter a baking sheet.

Combine the flour and salt in a large bowl. Cut ½ cup of the butter into ¼ inch thick slices and scatter on the top of the flour. Use a pastry cutter or two forks and cut the butter into the flour until the butter is in small pieces. Add the buttermilk, stirring until just combined.

Turn the dough out onto a floured cutting board or the cold counter and knead 3 or 4 times, adding additional flour if needed. Press or pat the dough into a ½-inch rectangle. Cut 8 to 12 biscuits with a biscuit cutter and place biscuits on the baking sheet, side by side and touching.

Bake 15 to 20 minutes until lightly browned. Brush the tops of the hot biscuits with the remaining 2 tablespoons of butter. Serve warm with jam or Chocolate Gravy (recipe below).

INGREDIENTS FOR CHOCOLATE GRAVY

1 cup sugar
1 tablespoon unsweetened cocoa powder
1 tablespoon self-rising flour (Note: If you can get it, use White Lily)
Pinch of salt
1 ¼ cups water
¼ teaspoon pure vanilla extract
1 tablespoon unsalted butter

DIRECTIONS

Combine sugar, cocoa powder, flour and salt in saucepan. Stir in 1 ¼ cups of water and the vanilla extract and bring to a boil over medium heat, stirring occasionally, until thick, about 15 minutes. Remove from heat and stir in butter. Serve warm. Makes about 1 ½ cups.

LEE J. COBB

It was during the making of *The Man Who Loved Cat Dancing* that I met Lee J. Cobb. He just happened to be one of my favorite actors. His cinematic performances in *Twelve Angry Men* and *On The Waterfront*, as well as *Death of a Salesman* on Broadway, were astounding.

Lee and I hit it off right away, and I was mesmerized with the car he had driven all the way from LA to St. George, Utah. It was a Maserati. He loved to drive fast cars and used any excuse to take it out on the road. He offered to take me out for a spin. It was a beautiful driving machine that took the mountainous curves of Zion National Park in stride at speeds of eighty to ninety miles per hour. As a way to thank him for the ride, I washed the car and shined the chrome one day while he was filming. He was completely surprised and delighted. That day began a friendship that lasted for many years.

Lee was a very interesting man who had an extraordinary life. He adored his wife, Mary, and their two musically talented sons. His vices were gambling and good cigars. He was passionate about good films and good acting. I remember how animated he was when he ran the movie *Mean Streets* for me at his modest home in Woodland Hills. He predicted wonderful futures for Martin Scorsese and Robert De Niro.

Although Lee played many villains and bad guys, he was one of the wittiest guys I have ever known. I was present for these first two anecdotes. They are true in every aspect.

Lee liked to do things on the spur of the moment.

I was lazing about in my room in Gila Bend, Arizona, watching a game show on TV when the phone rang.

"Hello."

"Where are you dining for lunch today, young Jim?"

"Haven't a clue."

"Meet me outside in five minutes. We're going to Buckeye, Arizona."

"Where's that?"

"About twenty-five minutes away."

"Okay."

I learned that Buckeye was due north on AZ-85 around forty minutes away. I also learned that the Maserati could go 135 miles per hour.

"Aren't you worried about getting a ticket?"

"Who could catch us? Listen to her purr."

"You're crazy!"

"I'm not the crazy one. You're the one riding in a car

Now that's a nice hat! *Attack on Terror*, 1975. *Author Collection.*

going 135 miles per hour, driven by a guy with a heart condition. Smell that leather! Why can't Detroit build a car like this?"

Buckeye was a charming place with a town square and a city café that served a blue-plate special. The café was full of farmers, ranchers, and blue-collar working stiffs. Lee called my attention to an older man who was eating English peas with a dinner knife. He would load them up in a row on the knife, ferry them to his mouth and expertly deposit them on his tongue without dropping a single pea. Lee was rapt with admiration.

"You always look for this kind of thing. You watch people. You might find just what you are looking for in a role you are playing. I've heard of this eating peas with a knife before, but until today I'd never seen it."

After pie and coffee we took a little stroll around the square. Lee was expansive. He saw a sign that said "Haberdashery." He got so excited over that. He said he hadn't seen that word since he was a boy. His father had a friend who was a haberdasher. We had to go in there. He definitely had to buy something from that haberdasher.

We were the only customers. Lee caught sight of some golf hats. Not golf "caps" like we golfers wear now, but a regular, fedora shaped, floppy sort of hat. He checked the price. It was marked at two dollars. Everybody loves a bargain. Lee began trying them on. Although there was a mirror, he checked my reaction every time he tried one on.

"What do you think of this one, Jim?"

"Fine, Lee. Looks good."

"Nah, I think the brim is too stingy."

"What do you think of this one?"

"Fine."

"Nah, I don't like the color."

We went through this routine five or six more times. The hats were all basically the same—one size, two colors, light blue and light yellow with black hat bands. You would think he was buying a tux to meet the queen. Finally he chose one, and we approached the counter. Lee paid for it and decided to wear it out of the store. He lit a cigar. Life was good. The owner and operator of the haberdashery then spoke to me as if Lee weren't even present.

"You know who that guy looks like?"

"No," I answered. "Who?"

"You know! That guy on TV!"

Lee just stood there adjusting his hat, ignoring the whole conversation. I was starting to enjoy this but I couldn't figure out where it was going. I tried to help.

"You mean the guy on *The Virginian?*"

"No! You know, it was a play on TV."

"*Death of a Salesman?*"

"Yeah! That was it!"

"So, you mean Lee J. Cobb?"

"That's him! Maybe it is him. Hey, mister. Are you Lee J. Cobb?"

Lee blew a couple of smoke rings before he replied, "Would Lee J. Cobb wear a two-dollar hat?"

We climb into the Maserati and Lee gives the haberdasher, who hasn't moved from his doorway, a regal wave as we say adieu to Buckeye.

On the way back to Gila Bend, Lee didn't attempt to set a new land speed record. We almost dawdled as the speedometer needle rarely passed ninety or so. He was in a storytelling mood, and he told me one about the time he was taping *Death of a Salesman* at CBS Fairfax. The cast was breaking for lunch, so Lee strolled over to the Hollywood Ranch Market to grab a bite at any number of ethnic eateries. He settled on an open stool at the counter of one of the sandwich joints. When the waitress brought him a glass of water and a menu she looked startled, then smiled knowingly, and winked. Lee didn't think much of it and turned his attention to the pastrami-on-rye special on the menu. The smiling waitress walked over to another waitress and the following "stage whisper" dialogue ensued:

Waitress Number 1: "Look over my shoulder. See the guy sitting at the counter?"

Waitress Number 2: "Yeah, so?"

Waitress Number 1: "Don't you know who that is?"

Waitress Number 2: (shrugs, shakes her head)

Waitress Number 1: "Sure you do! Take another look."

Waitress Number 2: (Takes another look) "Nope."

Waitress Number 1: (Exasperated) "That's Raymond Burr!"

Waitress Number 2: (Looks once more) "He wishes he was!"

LESLIE NIELSEN

Here's a guy who went from leading man to funny man—and I do mean funny. I worked with him when he guest starred on *Evening Shade* and will forever associate him with—dare I say it?—farting.

As a special gift, Leslie presented each of us writers and producers with a contraption he had made from some wire, a washer, and a rubber band. You'd twist it, stick it under your fanny, and then lift up one of your butt cheeks. It would then make the most delicious fart sound I'd ever heard.

Every day, we'd sit around the writer's room at a big table working and reworking the show's script for the

Leslie Nielsen with the *Evening Shade* writers. *Author Collection.*

Leslie Nielsen's Rootin Tootin Baked Beans

INGREDIENTS

1 pound pinto beans

1 medium onion, peeled and chopped

3 bay leaves

5 strips bacon, cut into thirds

½ cup orange juice

1 cup raisins

1 teaspoon chili powder

½ teaspoon cayenne pepper

½ cup molasses

1 jalapeño, fresh or canned

1 cup honey

½ cup brown sugar

¼ cup cider vinegar

1 28-ounce can crushed tomatoes

Salt and pepper to taste

DIRECTIONS

In the morning, cover the beans with water in a large cooking pot and allow to soak all day. At night, add enough warm water to cover the beans by three inches. Add the onion, bay leaves and bacon. Cover the pot and place into the oven at 250 degrees to cook overnight (about 8-10 hours). In the morning, drain off some of the cooking water so the beans are just barely covered. Add all the remaining ingredients and return to the oven for 4 hours. Enjoy! Then open a window.

week. We'd do a read with the cast and then tweak it some more. Every afternoon, about the same time, the UPS guy would come around for the pick-up and delivery for the day. We saw his next visit as a prime opportunity for us to test our new equipment.

There were ten or fifteen of us gathered around the table that day, including Leslie. The anticipation of the appearance of our unsuspecting victim was excruciating. When he finally arrived, we were cocked and loaded. He crossed the room and, as he did every day, picked up packages and envelopes left for him, and delivered some as well. When he finished his business and turned to leave, we struck. As he walked by, each of us in turn, never looking up from our scripts and with a straight face, would let go, appearing to never notice the cacophony of rumbles reverberating through the room. By the time the poor fellow got to the door, he was running. However, he was not quite fast enough to escape the final blast emitted by our darling little production assistant who was sitting by the door. Ah, life is sweet.

I still have my fart machine. It's in my desk drawer and I love to drive my wife crazy with it every once in a while. Boys will be boys.

LIZ ASHLEY

Liz played Marilu Henner's aunt on *Evening Shade*. She is talented, gorgeous, and outspoken.

One morning I had arrived to work particularly early and was on the soundstage working on a script. Other than a young female production assistant, no one else was around. I heard Liz come in, and she begin to chat with the young woman who was lamenting about her failed marriage. There was a profusion of sniffles. Liz listened intently, not saying a word. After the weeping had subsided, Liz lit a cigarette, took a long drag, and bestowed this comforting piece of advice, "Oh hell honey, husbands are like pancakes. You always have to throw the first one away."

Liz Ashley's "First Husband" Pancakes (A Little Spicy—Like Liz!)

INGREDIENTS

1 cup flour
1 tablespoon sugar
1 teaspoon salt
3 teaspoons baking powder
¼ teaspoon Allspice
¼ teaspoon nutmeg
¼ teaspoon cinnamon
¼ teaspoon ground cloves
1 egg
1 cup whole milk
2 tablespoons melted butter

DIRECTIONS

Sift all dry ingredients together. Beat egg with milk and mix together with the dry ingredients, whisking well until just blended. Add the melted butter. Cook up on a greased, well-heated griddle. Makes 8-10 pancakes.

NOTE: You don't *have* to throw the first one away…

MAMIE VAN DOREN

I was fortunate to work with a lot of beautiful women. Smart, beautiful women. Mamie Van Doren was one of them. We starred together in a production of *Will Success Spoil Rock Hunter?* along with Rick Jason at The Arlington Park Theater near Chicago. I had acted there before in a production of *The Rainmaker* as well as in a production of *The Tender Trap* with Burt and loved the venue. It was an old place, built in the 1930s, with a lot of character. They had both live productions and movies there.

One night, we were doing a scene in which Mamie's character, Rita Marlowe, is getting a massage. She was lying on a massage table wearing nothing but a towel. The scene was moving along as usual when Mamie suddenly "went up." That's a term we actors use when someone forgets their lines. For those of us used to working in live theater, another actor can sometimes help his fellow actor recover by inserting a line, in character, that might prompt the forgotten line. Before anyone on stage could try this tactic, Mamie was up off the table, sashaying over to Rick and me. Hugging her tiny pink towel, she announced to us that we were all going to "go back to page forty-nine."

Huh? She pointed to me and continued, " . . . and Jimmy, you say blah blah blah, and then Rick, you say blah blah blah." Rick shot me a look, and I thought he was going to run. The audience was silent. Then, just as adorable as you please, Mamie hopped back up on

Lucky me and Mamie Van Doren. *Author Collection.*

the table and started with her first line at the beginning of the scene. Aha! We got it! The audience got it! They went barmy with delight! We all realized then and there that Mamie had a photographic memory. Envisioning it in her mind, she was simply flipping the script back a few pages so that we could start over. There was a standing ovation at the end of that act.

I visited with Mamie at *The Hollywood Show* a few years back. She's still the same sweet, smart, beautiful bombshell of a girl that I remember.

The cast of *The Tender Trap* at The Arlington Park Theatre in Chicago. *Author Collection.*

Mamie Van Doren's Deeeeee-Lightful Doughnuts

INGREDIENTS FOR DOUGHNUTS

3 cups all-purpose flour
1 package dry yeast
½ teaspoon ground nutmeg
1 cup whole milk
¼ cup finely granulated white sugar
¼ cup vegetable oil
¾ teaspoon salt
1 egg
Lard for deep frying

DIRECTIONS

Combine 1 ½ cups of the flour, the yeast, and nutmeg. Combine the milk, sugar, vegetable oil, and salt, and heat in a saucepan until warm (do not boil). Add the liquid mixture to the dry ingredients and add the egg. Beat with an electric mixer on low speed for 30 seconds. Then beat a high speed for 3 minutes. By hand, stir in the remaining flour to make a soft dough.

Place dough in a greased bowl and turn once. Cover and chill.

Once chilled, place dough on lightly floured surface and let rest again for 10 minutes. Roll dough into an 18" x 12" rectangle. Cut with round biscuit or cookie cutter into doughnut shapes. Cover again and let rise for 30 minutes. Fry in deep, hot lard until golden, turning once. Drain and drizzle with sugar glaze.

Makes about 3 dozen.

INGREDIENTS FOR SUGAR GLAZE

2 cups powdered sugar
1 tablespoon melted butter
½ teaspoon vanilla
Scant milk

DIRECTIONS

Mix the powdered sugar with melted butter, vanilla, and just enough milk to make a thin glaze.

MARILYN MONROE

While I was in New York, my roommate and old friend from North Texas State College, Neal Weaver, told me this story:

A mutual friend of ours, Bill Basset, was attending classes at the Actor's Studio. Lee Strasberg was the teacher, and one day he informed the class that a new student would be joining. She was to be treated as any other student. No one was to make any fuss or to-do about her, and everything that took place in class was private and not to be discussed with anyone else, particularly the press. The new student was Marilyn Monroe.

Sure enough, the next day Marilyn Monroe showed up and found a seat near the back. As they were instructed, no one paid her any notice. Miss Monroe came incognito, as only she could. A simple silk scarf covered her famous tresses; jeans, sunglasses, and a $50,000 floor-length sable coat completed her disguise. Before long, the class became absorbed in the activities at the studio, and Marilyn was just one more famous face that had come to study under Strasberg.

A phone list was provided to the members of the studio so they might make arrangements to prepare a scene. One night fairly late, as Bill was almost asleep, his phone rang. He answered a little sleepily and slightly put out.

"Hello."

"Hello, Bill?"

It was unmistakably the unique, breathy voice of Marilyn Monroe. He was barely able to answer.

"Yes . . . "

"It's Marilyn."

There was a pause as Bill was speechless.

"You know, Marilyn . . . from class?"

MICHAEL JETER

Michael was one of those faultless actors who needed no direction. After the Monday table read, you could put him in wardrobe and shoot the show. *Evening Shade* filmed its shows on Friday nights in front of a live audience. Once when I was directing, we shot the first scene and then huddled with the writers and producers for their notes.

"He was a little campy," someone said, referring to Michael. The rest all nodded in agreement. It was my job to deliver the note and I wasn't sure how he would receive it.

Walking towards him, I was about two paces away when he looked up and asked, "Butch it up?"

I made a quick U-turn and muttered, "Yep, that's it."

I never had to give him another note.

Evening Shade writers. *Author Collection.*

PAUL LYNDE

One of the many nice things about having a regular part on a series is meeting the guest stars. *F Troop* was wonderful in that regard. Every week we had a top-notch guest star, and I had a whole week to get to know them and observe them up close. We had an array of the funniest people on the planet who were eager to be on the show because of the high ratings and the excellent writers. Also, many of the stars were personal friends of Forrest Tucker or Larry Storch, and they knew that they would have a lot of fun. A few of the stars that came through the Fort Courage gate were Milton Berle, George Gobel, Zsa Zsa Gábor, Harvey Korman, Vincent Price, Don Rickles, Henry Gibson, and of course no list would be complete without Paul Lynde.

It seems impossible to imagine that Paul passed on over a quarter of century ago. Anyone alive during the late 60s and 70s will remember him as the outrageous center box on *The Hollywood Squares* game show. Paul's droll but hilariously unpredictable answers to the questions posed by host Peter Marshall are legendary.

Peter: "Paul, in WWII, who was known as 'Old Blood and Guts'?"

Paul: "Barbara Stanwyck."

Peter: "Paul, why do Hell's Angels wear leather?"

Paul: "Because chiffon wrinkles."

Peter: "Paul, can you get an elephant drunk?"

Paul: "Yes, but she still won't go up to your apartment."

You get the idea.

Paul was booked on *F Troop* in an episode called "The Singing Mountie." Paul, as the Mountie, had come south on the trail of the Burglar of Banff (pronounced "Ban-phu-phu").

It was impossible not to laugh when Paul uttered the line, "We always get our man."

Naturally, we shot this episode in the middle of a summer heat wave. Poor Paul was in full dress as a Royal Canadian Mountie, including riding breeches, riding boots, heavy leather gloves, and the traditional red woolen tunic buttoned all the way to his chin. In those days, we didn't have plush air-conditioned mobile dressing rooms. What we had were folding canvas set chairs with our names on them. That was true for everyone, series stars and guest stars alike. It was a more democratic time.

It was wonderful being a part of a cast, just sitting around swapping stories between shots. We were expected to be ready when the camera was ready. When we shot on the Fort Courage set on the Warner Brothers back lot, we were exposed to the elements. In the early morning hours of January and February, it could get pretty nippy. I remember one such day when one of the horses relieved himself and left a large steaming pile of fertilizer. The craft services guy arrived with a shovel but complained that while it was steaming, the issue was technically the special effects department's problem.

This particular day was in July and it was hot. Africa hot. The property department had thoughtfully arranged our chairs in a straight line outside the bunkhouse to take advantage of what little shade there was from a porch overhang. We had shot the master of the singing Mountie's arrival at Fort Courage and it had taken awhile, as Paul Lynde was no cowboy. We had coverage to do and another scene involving the Mountie's departure. I believe there was more singing involved. The last scene we had done had just about sapped our strength, as we were being cooked alive. As the sun rose higher in the sky, it produced harsh shadows that could only be softened by adding reflectors and additional hot lights. We sat quietly awaiting the next shot as conversation at

Paul Lynde's "You Dumb Cluck" Chicken Salad

INGREDIENTS

4 chicken breasts, cooked and chopped

1 6-ounce can sliced black olives

1 small package slivered almonds

½ as much celery as chicken

½ cup mayo

¼ cup sour cream

Dash of Tabasco sauce

DIRECTIONS

Mix all the ingredients together and serve cold on a lettuce leaf, stuffed in a scooped-out tomato half, or on a sandwich.

that point took too much energy. All we could focus on was completing the day's work and cooling off at our favorite watering hole.

At that moment, three or four adults arrived, along with five or six kids. The kids were excitedly heading in our direction, waving autograph books. Paul let out a sort of strangled groan and closed his eyes. Warner Brothers wasn't like Universal. There were no buses full of tourists who paid to see a real movie studio. Nevertheless, there were occasional small groups like this one who knew some studio big shot and, as long as they didn't get in the way, we tried to be cordial because who knew if they were Jack Warner's grandkids or not.

Four of us were sitting in the deck chairs: Larry Storch in the first one, then me, then Paul, then Ken Berry. Forrest Tucker was in his golf cart in another patch of shade quietly sipping a scotch.

The kids were orderly and polite as their parents made sure they lined up and got each of our autographs in turn, except for Paul, who pretended to be sleeping. The first kid came through, got Larry's, got mine, looked at Paul, decided not to press the issue, skipped Paul, and got Ken's. The second and third kid did exactly as the first kid did. A precedent had been established.

I decided to have a little fun with Kid Number Four, so as I handed him his autograph book back, and before he could skip Paul, I said, "Hey, don't you want to get Mr. Lynde's autograph? It might be worth a lot of money someday."

Paul's eyes popped open and he shot me a withering glance. The kid looked at me, looked at Paul, shrugged, and thrust out his autograph book toward Mr. Lynde. Paul took it, but before he signed it, he locked eyes with Kid Number Four and said in that extraordinary delivery he was famous for, "You don't even know who I am, you dumb cluck!"

PAUL WILLIAMS

Paul Williams is one of the most prolific song-writers of all time, whose work includes a successful musical based on the *Happy Days* television series. He has won countless awards, and as of this printing, is president of the American Society of Composers, Authors, and Publishers. Nevertheless, some people will only remember him as Little Enos Burdette in the *Smokey and the Bandit* movies. You have to admit he was hilarious.

The difference in height between Paul (slightly over five feet) and his on-screen brother Pat McCormick (well over six feet) was a walking sight gag. Paul told me that Pat once announced to him, "From up here you look like an aerial photo of a human being."

My wife Mary and Paul Williams. *Author Collection.*

Paul Williams's "I'm No Shrimp" Casserole

INGREDIENTS

2 pounds fresh shrimp, cooked and deveined

2 cups white rice, cooked

1 cup mayonnaise

2 cups cream of chicken soup

1 package green onion dip mix

2 cups cheddar cheese, grated

DIRECTIONS

Combine all ingredients except cheese and mix together well. Pour into a casserole dish and top with cheese. Bake at 350 degrees for 30 minutes.

RICHARD DAWSON

Richard Dawson was one of the wittiest people I've ever known. You probably remember him as one of the stars of *Hogan's Heroes* or as the original kissing emcee of *Family Feud*. He told me this story when we were relaxing after a round of golf for a charity. I believe it to be true. You can make up your own mind. Here goes.

Dickie was married at one time to a beautiful British actress named Diana Dors. She got a lead in a movie to be shot in Hollywood. Since the movie was going to take four to six weeks, Diana decided to bring the children with her. Dickie was finishing a film in London, and the plan was for him to join his family in few days.

Everything went smoothly and Dickie was on a flight to LAX. It was a long flight, but those were the days when flying was a pleasure—plenty to eat and drink. I'm sure he was well cared for. This was, I believe, in the days when, thanks to Senator Joe McCarthy, our government was uncovering communists everywhere, especially in Hollywood. Laws were passed, and federal employees were on alert. At least travelers back then could keep their shoes on. In any case, nonresidents entering the US had to fill out a form with some pretty stupid questions on it. This one took the cake. It went something like this:

"While you are in the United States, do you plan or are you planning to overthrow the government by force or any other means?"

This was too much for Richard. His answer was, "Sole purpose of visit."

He was immediately sent back to England and wasn't allowed to enter the United States for another sixty days. His wife was not amused.

ROY ROGERS

I was lucky to work with several of my boyhood "heroes" of the big screen. The wonderful cowboy actor Bob Steele and I performed together on *F Troop*. The great Jimmy Stewart and I acted together on his television show *Hawkins on Murder*. And, I was so very fortunate to have the opportunity to work with Roy Rogers on his last movie, *Mackintosh and T.J.*, in 1975. It was a sweet Disney-esque style of film set in modern times about a cowboy drifter (Roy) who befriends a troubled teenager while working on a ranch. We mostly shot the film at the historic Four Sixes Ranch, a huge, working cattle ranch up in the Panhandle of Texas (if you are from Texas, you know where that is).

In this particular movie I play a not-so-nice fellow named Cotton who ends up in a fist fight with Roy's character, Mackintosh. A portion of our little scuffle occurred in water and, unfortunately, Roy caught some kind of amoeba and later developed a terrible stomach issue as a result. There can be some nasty little critters floating around in ranch ponds and streams. In any event, while working with Roy, I learned some fun facts about him that I didn't know.

Apparently, the King of the Cowboys loved to bowl. He had, for years, been an accomplished bowler and participated in numerous celebrity bowling tournaments. Production crews would scout out a bowling alley near the

How about them boots? *Author Collection.*

filming locations, and Roy would spend his off-time at the lanes. He was quite good, and we enjoyed knocking down some pins.

Also, I don't know if it was nerves, a ritual, or simply to clear his throat, but before each take Roy would yodel a bit. Yes, yodel. I had previously worked with Jack Lemmon on *The China Syndrome*, and, as everyone knew, he would say "It's magic time" before each scene. However, a yodel will catch you off guard if you aren't ready for it. I found it particularly funny and would often get the giggles (the milk coming out of your nose kind of giggles) and we'd have to cut before Roy ever got a line out of his mouth. Still, it seems appropriate for Roy to do, and now every time I watch him on one of his television shows or movies I can picture him yodeling away before the director yelled "Action." I still giggle.

Proud of my star on the Texas Trail of Fame in Fort Worth. *Author Collection.*

MARY TYLER MOORE

Mary Tyler Moore was one talented, hardworking lady. Early on in her career, she had some good roles in notable television shows in Hollywood such as *77 Sunset Strip*, *The Ozzie and Harriet Show*, and *Hawaiian Eye*, just to name a few. Then, she made her mark on *The Dick Van Dyke Show*. Who can ever forget perky Laura Petrie? Not long after that show ended another long-running hit with her own name in the title, *The Mary Tyler Moore Show*, was born. And she turned the world on with her smile for most of the 1970s. But what she really wanted was to have her own variety show. She got the chance in 1978 with *Mary*.

During the 1960s and 1970s variety shows seemed to dominate the small screen—*Donny & Marie, The Glen Campbell Goodtime Hour, The Dean Martin Show, Flip Wilson, Sonny and Cher*. My personal favorite was *The Carol Burnett Show*. Harvey Korman was a good pal, and I can't keep a straight face thinking about him. He and Tim Conway were the dynamic duo of comedy. And Carol? Well, she was Carol. Marvelous, funny, funny, funny Carol. Vicki Lawrence was just the right amount of icing the cake needed.

How I ever crossed the minds of the producers of *Mary*, I'll never know. As I've pointed out elsewhere in this book, I could neither sing nor dance. So, I can't imagine how I ever came up in conversation. To tell you the truth, I think my agent was as perplexed as I was. I was sure that a few minutes after entering "the room," the producers would see how foolish they had been for calling me in, and the casting lady would certainly be fired. I was feeling guilty before I even auditioned.

They must have seen something they liked because the next day my agent called to tell me I was part of an ensemble cast that included young performers David Letterman, Michael Keaton, Swoosie Kurtz, and Merrill Markoe, and veteran comedian Dick Shawn.

Mary was a darling and was always upbeat and encouraging. She really did have spunk. We sang and danced our little hearts out. We had a great time. We only lasted nine weeks.

Mary went on to earn an Oscar nomination and a Golden Globe win, as well as many more nominations and awards for her talent as an actress. Michael Keaton has had a dynamite career with his own Oscar nomination and Golden Globe Award, among others.. I never get tired of watching him and proudly admit that I'm a big *Gung Ho* fan. Swoosie Kurtz continued to take her Broadway talents to the big and small screens with much success. Merrill Markoe ended up with a wonderful writing career, winning Daytime and Primetime Emmys. Good old Dick went out the way a lot of actors would like to go—while performing on stage. But I wish we could have had more years of laughs with him. Of course, we all know what became of that entertaining young fellow David Letterman. During the last week of his show, David had Michael on as a guest. As they went down memory lane, they brought up *Mary* and me and the rest of the cast. I'm touched they remembered.

The cast of *The Mary Show*, 1978. *Author Collection.*

With funny man Tim Conway.
Courtesy of Frank John Pope.

```
cl  CBSINC LSA
    WUHO51    LSA393(1254)(4-036100E174)PD 06/23/78 1254
    ICS IPMBNGZ CSP
    5017325691 TDBN FORT SMITH AR 15 06-23 1254P EST
    PMS JAMES HAMPTON

    THE MARY SHOW, RDM REPORT DELIVERY BY MAILGRAM, DLR
    CBS STUDIOS FAIRFAX AT BEVERLY BLVD                    25
    LOS ANGELES CA
    CONGRATULATIONS TO YOU YOU ARE NOT OUR NUMBER TWO SON TODAY YOU ARE
    NUMBER ONE
       MOM AND DAD
    (IVAN H HAMPTON 616 NORTH 34TH ST FORT SMITH AR 72903)
    1227PDa
    CBSINC LSA
    KZ
```

Telegram from my folks, 1978. *Author Collection.*

MICHAEL CRAWFORD

I had a very short-lived career on *The Dukes of Hazzard*. (Don't worry, this eventually leads up to Michael Crawford.) When my old pal Jim Best, who played Sheriff Roscoe P. Coltrane on the show, decided to hold out for a raise in the second season, CBS called his bluff and replaced him with a number of "sheriffs of the week." I was one of them. My character, Sheriff Buster Moon, was well received, and the network booked me for nine episodes. However, when I saw Jim on the set the third day into my first week of shooting, I knew the standoff was over.

Sure enough, I was called into the studio offices with my agent and was told that Jim Best was indeed back to work. The network, however, wanted to offer me a plum role on a Duke's spinoff called *Enos*, which starred Sonny Shroyer. Sonny and I had both been in *The Longest Yard* back in the 1970s, and he was a good guy. I was to be Enos's sidekick. There was no question that I had made a nice living as a sidekick, but I just wasn't interested. The network was not amused at my decision, as they weren't looking forward to paying off my nine-episode contract. Never mind that I had insulted them by insinuating that just because a show is a spinoff of another popular show, it doesn't assure success. I couldn't help but remind them of a few of those duds. Not one of my wiser choices.

In the studio parking lot my agent wiped his sweaty brow and, in a trembling voice, announced that he wasn't sure that either of us would ever "work in this town again." I was stricken with the sudden realization that he was right, and we were both doomed. But at least I

Dukes of Hazzard star John Schneider and me.
Courtesy of Frank John Pope.

With Michael Crawford in *Condorman*. © 1981 Disney.

could look forward to nine more checks from CBS before I starved to death. Visions of me as a wino passed out on Clark Gable's star on the Hollywood Walk of Fame suddenly filled my brain. I have to say, however, that I enjoyed my quick stint on Dukes. I had worked with my old friend Denver Pyle again and made a new one in John Schneider. What a doll he is. An excellent actor too. I still see him at celebrity events every now and then, and he always comes by to hug my neck. So it wasn't a complete disaster.

Surprisingly, the day after I turned down the job on *Enos*, my agent, who I thought was not speaking to me, sent over a script for a Disney movie called *Condorman*. The first few words of the script were "Exterior—Eiffel Tower." That was all it took for me to accept the role. It was a fun action-adventure story about a comic-book artist who "becomes" the superhero he's created and ends up working with the CIA. The cast was a fine one consisting of Oliver Reed, Dana Elcar, Barbara Carrera, and Michael Crawford. (See, I told you we'd get to Michael

Crawford.) The picture was scheduled to be filmed in a number of different exciting locations like Paris, Monte Carlo, Zermatt, and Monaco. Even better!

Every actor has his own way of preparing for and working a role. Michael was an upbeat, interesting fellow who liked to rehearse. A lot. Personally, I felt better keeping things "fresh" and letting scenes develop naturally without going over it again and again. But in show business you learn to be accommodating to your fellow actors.

The opening scene in the movie begins with me photographing a man in a bird suit leaping from the Eiffel Tower. The man in the bird suit was Michael. His costume consisted of a brightly colored leotard with a heavy set of working wings strapped to his back. Yes, they actually flapped. Michael's character, Woody, ends up crashing into the Seine River, and my character, Harry, rushes in to pull him out. "Action!" was called, and I jumped in the water and started to swim. Neither the director, the crew, nor I was aware that Michael was actually being pulled under the water by the weight of the wings of his costume. Once in the river with him, I realized how hard he was struggling. After I had a good hold on him, I began to try to pull him free of the wings, but they had partially collapsed, making it more difficult to maneuver in the water. The two of us began to kick as hard as we could with Michael still strapped to the sinking costume. I had him with one arm while I worked toward the shore with the other. Surely, I thought, someone would come running. But, no. The cameras were rolling. No one was yelling "Cut." Then, it occurred to me . . . everyone thought we were acting. After all, we were very talented chaps, weren't we?

We finally managed to make it to the concrete edge of the river, thankful to be alive. That's when we finally heard "Cut!" and thunderous applause from our director and crew. "Bravo! Bravo!" they cheered. "We got that in one take!" our director announced. Thank God.

Another quick story about Michael. One night while we were in Zermatt, the phone in my hotel room rang around 3:00 a.m. It was Michael.

"Go look out the window," Michael said.

"What? Is this a joke?"

"No. Just go look out the window."

"Okay, but if this were anybody else but you . . ."

I flopped out of bed, went over to the window, and opened the curtains. The sun was just beginning to rise over the top of the Matterhorn. The rays were hitting the snow-covered peak of the mountain. So help me it looked like molten gold was flowing from the top of the Matterhorn. It was one of the most beautiful sights of nature I'd ever seen.

I never asked Michael what he was doing up at 3:00 a.m., but I was glad he was. Hats off to you lad!

Visiting Walt's place. *Author Collection.*

NINETEEN
THE LAST ACT

Although I didn't give up performing altogether, my job as a writer on *Evening Shade* in the early 1990s led me to another career—a sitcom director. Once again, Burt Reynolds would prove to be the common thread in the tapestry of my life in Hollywood.

I received a call from casting director Fran Bascom, who had recently cast me as the murdering, drug dealing Reverend Saul in the soap opera *Days of Our Lives* (I got a lot of hate mail playing that role). Fran was casting

Burt's sitcom, *Evening Shade*, and thought I'd be perfect for a character who was an old friend of Burt's character, Wood, in an episode where they were attending their thirtieth class reunion. I couldn't accept the offer fast enough.

The caliber of talent on the show was unbelievable. The actors: Charles Durning, Hal Holbrook, Ossie Davis, Michael Jeter, Marilu Henner, Liz Ashley, and Burt. The writers: Linda Bloodworth-Thomason, David Nichols, Thom Bray, Michael Ross, Don Rhymer, and Brent

With the remarkable Charles Durning. *Author Collection.*

Roger Clinton, President Bill Clinton, Burt Reynolds, and me relaxing on the set of *Evening Shade. Author Collection.*

Forever grateful to my pal Harry Thomason. *Author Collection.*

At President Bill Clinton's birthday bash. *Author Collection.*

Briscoe, to name a few. The producers: Harry Thomason, Victor Fresco, Lamar Jackson, Doug Jackson, and on and on. Greatness. Just greatness.

I had a wonderful time that week and was happy to be back in touch with Burt. Shortly thereafter, thanks in part to Marilu Henner's enthusiasm over my joke-telling on set, I was offered a writing gig on the show. I couldn't believe it. It was unheard of for someone my age to be a rookie writer on a hit sitcom. But there I was. Have I mentioned how lucky I've been?

Our executive producer, Harry Thomason, is a laid-back Southern gentleman and one heck of a good guy. We remain great friends to this day. We've certainly had a lot of laughs. Honestly, I think Harry liked me because I was just about the only person who would fly in his plane with him. We'd just zoom off to Catalina or someplace for lunch and leave everyone else in our dust. Thank God for Depends.

One day, Harry asked me to direct an episode of the show. He and Linda were busy with soon-to-be President Bill Clinton's campaign, and they were traveling quite a bit. I said yes, and that was the beginning of the next ten years of my life as a television director, starting at the age of fifty-six. Oh, and I got to meet my first president too. He really can play that saxophone.

I went on to direct many other episodes of *Evening Shade* as well as other sitcoms including *Grace Under Fire*, *Sister Sister*, *Smart Guy*, *The Tony Danza Show*, *Boston Common*, and *Hearts Afire*, until I officially retired and moved back to Texas with my bride, Mary.

Since then, I have continued to play golf in celebrity tournaments all over the United States. Once, I bowled in a fundraiser with President George W. Bush. He's a super nice fellow with a great sense of humor! I wish we would have gotten matching bowling shirts! I also attended Louise Mandrell's celebrity clay pigeon shoot several times. That was a lot of fun, and I must say I was relieved to see that Vice President Cheney wasn't invited. Whew! In any event, these types of events have afforded me the opportunity to continue to see old friends from Hollywood and elsewhere, as well as to make new ones. Sometimes, in high places!

I've also enjoyed meeting my fans and reuniting with my actor pals at various celebrity conventions such as western festivals, sci-fi and horror conventions, nostalgia television conventions, and comic cons. I have a ball. If you've never been to one, it should be on your bucket list. I am always humbled by the love and kindness my fans show me. Folks from as far away as Belgium, Spain, Germany, and Japan have come just to see me. I'm always touched by comments like "When I was a kid my dad worked a lot but we always spent Tuesday nights together watching *F Troop*." Or, "You

President George W. Bush, First Lady Laura Bush, and me.
Courtesy of Andrew Slaton.

Directing on the set of *Sister Sister* with Tia and Tamara Mowry.
Author Collection.

Directing on the set of *Smart Guy* with Tahj Mowry.
Author Collection.

remind me so much of my own father. When I watch *Teen Wolf*, it's like watching him." And "I enjoyed watching you in . . . well, everything!". Other people will, in an affectionate way, refer to me by a character's name. "Hey Dobbs!" "How you doing Caretaker?" "Hi Mr. Howard!"

I like to think of it as delayed applause.

Thanks from the bottom of my heart, everybody.

Now get outta here, and let me miss you!

With the talented singer Gary Morris. *Author Collection.*

Cowboy poet, actor, and singer Red Steagall, me, and Coach Darrell Royal. *Author Collection.*

Golf tournament gang with comedian Jimmy Labriola, Dennis Hopper, and Robert Loggia, and friend. *Author Collection.*

The Par 3 Band: Richard Karn, me, John Cafferty (Beaver Brown Band), Jimmi Jamison (Survivor), a fellow musician, and Jack McGee. *Author Collection.*

Caught me with my britches down! *Author Collection.*

Golf madness with actors Michael Storm and Marc McClure. *Author Collection.*

My wife, Mary, and me hanging out with comedian Henry Cho and his wife, Amy. *Author Collection.*

Pro golfer Rich Beam and me. *Author Collection.*

With buddy Ernest Borgnine. *Author Collection.*

With my talented pal Scott Wilson. *Author Collection.*

With *Hill Street Blues* actor and ex-NFL player Ed Marinaro. *Author Collection.*

Song man Jimmie Rodgers and me. *Author Collection.*

Me and my cigar. *Author Collection.*

ACKNOWLEDGMENTS

To say writing this book was a labor of love would not be quite accurate. It was really just a lot of labor. I had been telling stories about the people I'd worked with over the years to anyone who would listen at dinner parties, celebrity events, and other gatherings. Many of my friends had encouraged me to write them down, but it wasn't until my wife bought the cattle prod that I actually began to write this book in earnest. I'm so glad she married me.

I'll never be able to compose a list of *all* of the people who have been so valuable to me as an actor and as a human being, but these deserve special recognition.

Thank you to my parents, Edna and Ivan Hampton. I really appreciate you not sending me to the nuns or military school (which you threatened to do on many occasions). To my brother Blake, your success was always an inspiration to me. Memories of my brother Dan, the rodeo clown and cowboy, have always brought a smile to my face.

To my children, Andrea, Jimmy, and Frankie, who are grown with families of their own, I hope there's always laughter in your lives. You've certainly brought laughter to mine.

Thanks to my in-laws, Ko and Bill David, for welcoming me into your family and introducing me to kimchi.

Where would we be without good teachers in our lives? I am so grateful to Frances Paar, Perry Fite, Mary McCormic, and Michael Howard. I am confident that their care and guidance have been instrumental in making the lives of their students that much better.

My gratitude goes to those casting directors, producers, and directors from my early days in Hollywood who gave a skinny kid from Texas a fighting chance: Jim Lister, Ruth Burch, Charles Rondeau, and Christian Nyby, just to name a few. Thanks for having faith in me.

To my first agents, Paul and Walter Kohner at The Kohner Agency, the lovely Nina Nisenholtz at William Morris, and my manager and friend Larry Kubik, I appreciate all of your hard work so that I could make a living doing something I love.

Would any of this have happened without my pal Burt Reynolds? I don't think so. I'll always be indebted to you, buddy.

I would be remiss not to give a heartfelt thanks to some of the other wonderful actors I've had the opportunity to work with: Jimmy Stewart, Doris Day, Rock Hudson, James Garner, Michael Crawford, Jack Lemmon, Jane Fonda, Michael Douglas, and Billy Bob Thornton. I've learned so much from all of you.

To Pat Boone and his late, sweet wife Shirley, thanks for all of the prayers and support. I've been blessed to have had you in my life.

From the bottom of my heart, I want to thank the beautiful, talented, and fabulous Adriana Trigiani. Your enthusiasm gave me the courage to put my thoughts and memories on paper. I'll be forever grateful.

Thank you to Harry Thomason and Linda Bloodworth-Thomason for giving a fifty-six-year-old writer his first directing gig. I ended up with a whole second career. You were (and are) my favorite team to work with. Didn't we all have fun with Leslie Nielsen's fart machine?

Buck and Kim Pate, Jim Bob and Esther Baugh, Paul and Rosanne Hunt, April Slaughter, and Mike Marchetti, your friendship and support are priceless.

Andy, Ernie, Tim, Tom, Mrs. Coakley's oldest boy (you know who you are John Paul), and all my buddies who take one day at a time, you make me remember that good friends are more valuable than gold.

Finally, thank you to my wife Mary, who helps me every day in every way. You are the love of my life.

Oh, and I'll take those dance lessons now.